REVISED EDITION

GOING OFF THE GRID

THE HOW-TO BOOK OF SIMPLE LIVING AND HAPPINESS

GARY COLLINS, MS

SECOND NATURE PUBLISHING

Albuquerque, NM

THE SIMPLE LIFE OFF GRID SERIES (BOOK 1)
Going Off The Grid: The How-To Book of Simple Living and Happiness
(Second Edition)

© 2017, 2021 by Gary Collins

For information about special discounts for bulk purchasing, and/or direct inquiries about copyright, permission, reproduction and publishing inquiries, please send an email to: contact@thesimplelifenow.com

Printed in the United States of America

Second Nature Publishing
Albuquerque, NM 87109
www.thesimplelifenow.com

CONTENTS

GOING OFF THE GRID

Get Your Free Goodies!

Get Your Free Goodies and Be a Part of My Special Community!

Building a solid relationship with my readers is incredibly important to me. It's one of the rewards of being a writer. From time to time, I send out an email to what I call "The Simple Life Insider's Circle" (never spammy, I promise) to keep you up to date with special offers and information about anything new I may be doing. I've moved away from using social media in the pursuit of a simpler life, so if you want to be part of the "in crowd", The Simple Life Insider's Circle is the place to be.

If that's not enough enticement, when you sign up, I'll send you some spectacular free stuff!

- 10 Steps for Achieving Your Off-The-Grid Dream
- The Five Simple Life Success Principles Printout
- Free chapter of *The Simple Life Guide To Decluttering Your Life*
- Free chapter of *The Simple Life Guide To Financial Freedom*
- 10% off and free shipping on your first order at The Simple Life website.

You'll get these goodies when you sign up to be a part of The Simple Life Insider's Circle at:

http://www.thesimplelifenow.com/offgridresources

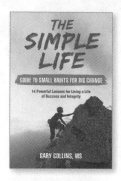

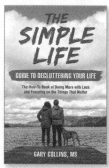

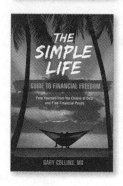

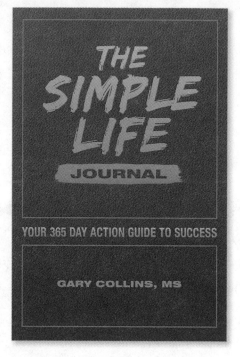

BOOKS BY GARY COLLINS

The Simple Life Journal

Your 365 Day Action Guide to Success
(sold only at www.thesimplelifenow.com)

The Simple Life Guide to Small Habits for Big Change

14 Powerful Lessons for Living a Life of Success
and Integrity

The Simple Life Guide to Decluttering Your Life

The How-to Book of Doing More with Less and
Focusing on the Things That Matter

The Simple Life Guide to Financial Freedom

Free Yourself from the Chains of Debt and Find
Financial Peace

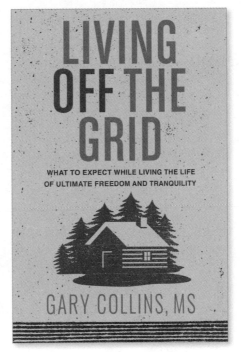

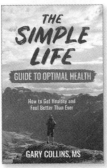

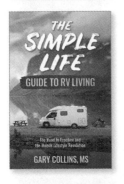

REVISED EDITION

GOING OFF THE GRID

THE HOW-TO BOOK OF SIMPLE LIVING AND HAPPINESS

*In the spirit of simplifying my life and my business,
I have set up a webpage with all of the photos
of my off-grid projects at:*

www.thesimplelifenow.com/offgridpics

INTRODUCTION

People who read this book end up in one of two groups. The first group is made up of readers who follow the advice in this book and discover just how peaceful and liberating this lifestyle can be. The second group is made up of readers who realize that what they're *really* after is something I call "The Simple Life". Both groups are perfectly fine, and my books help both types of people. My *Going Off the Grid* books are for the first group, and my *Simple Life* books and products are for the other. Either way, this book will be the first part of your journey towards a *Better Life*. It will also help you discover which group you belong in, and more importantly, how to get there.

So, if you're ready for a better life away from all the noise and clutter of "The Grid", you've picked the right book. Let me say that this book is NOT about disappearing from society, living in a shack without running water, eating squirrels, or prepping yourself for a post-apocalyptic world where you hoard baked beans and hunt zombies with a shotgun and a chainsaw. This is a book about my adventure and how I did it by living a (somewhat modern) lifestyle off-the-grid. It's not about disappearing. Believe me, I used to work for the federal government in Military Intelligence and Law Enforcement—and I can tell you that if you think you are going to live 100 percent off-the-grid where "they" can't bother you . . . good luck with that!

Not to say, what I have done and do is easy—it is not. Compared to most people in the modern world, I live a very different lifestyle. Yes, I do cut down trees, split my own firewood, work with my hands, and spend a great deal of time outdoors. But I don't want to have my lifestyle confused with someone who is living without basic modern necessities, making their own clothes, their own soap, growing all their own food, living just a step away from a primitive troglodyte. I know people like this, and I applaud them, but this is not the life I was looking for when going off-the-grid. I wanted to find a balance between minimal modern technology and a simpler way of living. I believe this is what most people are aspiring to find today—a life of simple peace and sanity. If you're one of those people, this book has everything you need to get started. I like to call this lifestyle "one foot in, one foot out". It's about enjoying all the benefits of modern progress and technology, minus the noise and the drama. If you've read *The Simple Life* books, you already know why this lifestyle is so appealing. If not, I'm glad you started your journey with this book.

To say a great deal has changed in my life since 2010, when I first started seriously working on my plan to live off-the-grid, would be an understatement. The first edition of this book was started around 2014, at the time of this (second edition), it's 2020. Not only have things changed in my personal life since I first started this adventure, my entrepreneurial endeavors now include a new company, website, podcast, multiple books on off-grid-living: *The Simple Life* books series and *The Simple Life Journal,* with much more to come. Even though this book has continued to be a best-seller, I felt it was time to give this book a well-deserved update.

For you who are new to me and to The Simple Life, this was a book I never intended to write. When I started planning a more remote lifestyle, while still working in the federal government as a Special Agent, I never intended to share my adventure with the public. It was just something I wanted to do on my own. No snazzy marketing campaigns, no "look at me I think I'm cool" or invitations to partake in social media voyeurism. It was just me living my life. Then something changed my mind. It all started when I was a guest on a podcast discussing Primal Health, which was the focus of my business after leaving the government. This was around 2011 or 2012 (I was doing a lot of podcast appearances back then). At the end of the interview, the host asked: "Do you have any new projects going on at the moment?" Nonchalantly, I replied: "I just bought twenty-acres, and I plan to build a house off-the-grid." Little did I know that not only my life, but my life-purpose would be heading in a very different direction because of that statement.

You'll find the details of how I got to this point in my book *The Simple Life Guide to Decluttering Your Life*. For now, my point is that the response to this simple announcement was overwhelming and life changing. My email inbox was flooded with people asking how I was going about my "off-the-grid project". Oh boy, I didn't see any of that coming!

Luckily, I had just bought my land and finished the first road to the future building site. So, when I say that this book idea came out of nowhere . . . well, it did. That's when I realized I needed to document this project and share as much as I could. I had no idea people were interested in such a lifestyle, because all my friends thought I was a bit off my rocker when I first told them. I thought it was just something "natural" to seek a simpler and more remote life away from all the noise and clutter. I was completely burned out with life (being told who and what I was supposed to be) and living in congested areas. I wanted to get back to the basics and figure out what happiness was to me, instead of just following the "widget in, widget out" model sold to me by mainstream society.

Simply put, I told my going off-the-grid story as it really happened. No fluff, no BS. I documented my adventure, sharing all the good and all the bad. As I have explained in my *Simple Life* books, the real lessons came when things didn't go the way I expected. That stupid thing called adversity—which it appears many people try to avoid these days—is where the real gold is. What is the point of me just sharing all my triumphs and successes? Why not just share the good stuff and give you all the shortcuts to going off-the-grid and living The Simple Life? Ah, that is the problem today; everyone wants all the joys out of life without putting in the hard work.

Many self-help authors prey on our need to avoid adversity. I call these authors the "False Prophets", and they are everywhere. What they won't tell you is that life just doesn't work that way. I always give it to you straight, no matter how stupid I may look at times. And trust me; I can be a top winner of the stupid award. But that's okay, because I just dust myself off, give a little chuckle and get back to it. I'd be doing you a disservice by saying you can shortcut that process. Adversity and failure are a necessary part of learning and eventually succeeding.

I have been pleasantly surprised by the positive feedback I've received from this "never meant to be written" book. The fact that I have helped thousands of people pursue their dream of escaping the "Cult of Clutter" and living off-the-grid is humbling, to say the least. Heck, I even have neighbors who read my book and started their journey into The Simple Life. Yes, a little creepy, but so far none of them have shown up at my doorstep (don't get any ideas).

The one thing I want to be as clear as I can about—I have never called myself, or even thought of myself as the guru of living off-the-grid, nor would I want to be considered so. I've simply shared, and continue to share my story, because people are interested in it. Living off-the-grid is highly unique to the individual or group doing it; no one does it the same. I just provide my knowledge and experience to those who want it. I don't preach, "My way is the only way." This is your journey, so you need to find your own path in this adventure. And trust me, it will be an adventure!

That said, I'm not shy in giving my opinion on certain aspects of going off-the-grid and living off-the-grid. Can I come off a little preachy at times? Sure, especially when I take shots at the phony False Prophets who write about this topic, but still live in their downtown studio apartment or their parents' spare bedroom. But I don't attack these fake authors to be an asshole. I do it because I hate seeing readers led astray by imposters. Everything I do in *The Simple Life* is about helping people. For some, this just isn't their flavor, and I get that, but I hope if this is the case, you are still able to get some life nuggets from reading my books.

Since going off-the-grid is ultimately the final stretch of the full journey towards living The Simple Life, I include descriptions of my Five Simple Life Principles throughout my books. These principles are your compass for staying on track during your off-the-grid adventure. . . .

- Knowledge is power
- Avoid extremes
- Keep it simple
- Something is better than nothing
- Take action today and every day

If you want to dive deeper into these Principles, go to my website and grab any one of my *Simple Life* books. If you've got a lot of obstacles (financial problems, health problems, excess clutter etc.) standing in the way of getting to this life, start with *The Simple Life Guide to Decluttering Your Life*. If you're looking to get your toe in before you go big, grab my shorter book *Life Balance Reboot*. Those books are the best introduction to The Simple Life. Remember that your first mission is to figure out which of the two above mentioned groups you belong in.

For my final point (and this may surprise a lot of people), I hope you don't agree with everything I say. In my book *The Simple Life Guide to Small Habits for Big Change*, I talk about walking to the beat of your own drum. This is an essential ingredient of living The Simple Life—being true to yourself instead of blindly following others. As you read this, and my other books, I encourage you to question everything and come to your own conclusions. This isn't a one-way street—I have also learned a great deal from people who have read my books and who follow me. And for that, I'm grateful and feel incredibly lucky to share my journey with you.

1

What This Book Will (and Won't) Do for You

How far off-the-grid do you want to go? Living without the convenience of public utilities has great rewards but also many challenges. Going off-the-grid also means different things to different people. There is no official definition of the term, and many variations of off-grid living prevail. Here are a few of the various ways you can enjoy the off-the-grid lifestyle:

LIVING OFF-THE-GRID: As I define it, means creating a home that is autonomous and does not rely on public utility connections, such as electricity, water, waste management, sewers, gas lines, and telecommunication and internet services delivered via cables. Most off-grid homes are in rural areas, but not all of them. As you will discover in this book, living off-the-grid doesn't mean living like a caveman or Tibetan monk. You can be off-the-grid and still have a phone, internet connection, modern toilet and shower, and appliances. You can still live in a comfortable, warm, up-to-date home. It just takes the proper planning, which is what this book is all about. In other words, living off-the-grid is more about living away from the clutter, noise, and the drama of "The Grid", a term I'll explain in detail later.

LIVING SEMI-OFF-THE-GRID: Means the use of one or several public utilities, but not all of them. Some rural homes are semi-off-the-grid out of necessity. For example, many houses in remote locations have public electrical services but also a self-contained (off-grid) well and/or septic system. This is the type of living I experienced while growing up. A semi-off-the-grid approach works well for people who need a guaranteed utility service to survive, such as someone using medical devices that require a reliable source of electricity but who still want to be as independent of regular utility services as possible.

Whether your goal is to go completely or partially off-the-grid, this book will show you the way. This book will be of great use to anyone who wants to transition to a modern and comfortable yet fully or partially off-the-grid lifestyle. I wrote it primarily for people who prefer to hire contractors to help them build, rather than those who want to eke out an existence using only what the land provides. So, if you want to live autonomously but still enjoy modern creature comforts and telecommunications, this book will be an excellent resource and, I hope, help you avoid many costly and frustrating mistakes during your off-grid adventure.

What You WON'T Find in This Book

LIVING PRIMITIVE-OFF-THE-GRID: Is for people who prefer to espouse a more primitive style of off-the-grid living, opting to live more like our great-grandparents might have. For example, they might live in a tiny cabin *without any electricity or running water* and make their own supplies and structures out of the trees and rocks present on their land. It's almost like camping, but with permanent structures, usually built by hand by the people who will live in them. This book is not for people looking for this kind of lifestyle.

HOMESTEADING: Living a self-sufficient lifestyle, sometimes in conjunction with living off-the-grid. Homesteaders live in a manner similar to our ancestors who had farms. They grow their own food, preserve foodstuffs for cold seasons, and often raise animals and/or hunt for meat. Some homesteaders build modern off-grid homes and have cars, computers, and so on. If you don't want to have to go to the grocery store ever again, and the idea of hobby farming appeals—homesteading may be of interest to you. However, it's not the focus of this book.

Main point: You can be a homesteader and not live off-grid. You can also live off-the-grid without being a homesteader—which is what I do. I know people who live in one form or other of these variants above. Again, it boils down to what type of lifestyle you are looking for—there is no right or wrong answer.

PREPPING: A lifestyle carried out by "preppers". Preppers believe in preparing for the future and anticipating how to handle a major threat to life or disaster, either natural or man-made. Acquiring survival skills (such as homesteading), stocking survival supplies, and being able to live without the benefits of a utility grid are usually a part of this lifestyle. I believe everyone should be able to choose their own lifestyle, and certainly there are many people who incorporate elements of several off-grid options into their homes. For example, many off-grid enthusiasts dabble in homesteading or prepping to some degree.

However, this book will *not* cover subjects related to primitive off-grid living, homesteading, or prepping in any detail. If you want to undertake one of these options, you can use this book for some planning ideas in conjunction with other resources that focus exclusively on these topics.

SURVIVALISTS: This group is sometimes confused with preppers or prepping, but they are a little different. Survivalists consider themselves individuals who can live in nature after a natural disaster, or after getting lost, during a "grid-down situation", or just for fun. Survivalists can build a basic shelter, start a fire, gather and hunt their own food using primitive tools that are usually made from items they find in nature. You will often hear the term "bushcraft" thrown around describing the skills survivalists have and use. Again, living this kind of lifestyle is not the focus in this book.

As you can see, there is a lot of terminology and a lot of variations of off-grid living. Some of the more hardcore preppers, homesteaders, or survivalists might even insist that their way is the only "true" way to live off-the-grid. Most people will mix and match one or more of the above lifestyles to create the lifestyle they want to live. Again, there are no steadfast rules as far as I'm concerned. But I wanted to familiarize you with the above options, as they are often mentioned when talking about living an off-the-grid lifestyle. There are numerous books on the topics mentioned above. If you're interested in adding them to your off-the-grid adventure, I highly recommend you research some of them. But again, the above topics will not be discussed in this book.

So, to be clear, my definition of living off-the-grid is creating a home that is autonomous and does not rely on public utility connections, such as electricity, water, waste management, sewers, gas lines, and telecommunication and internet services delivered via cables. If that's your goal, this book is absolutely the best guide you can get your hands on.

The Realities of Off-The-Grid Home Building

If you are still reading, it's because you want to live independently of public utilities but still be in a modern and comfortable home. You probably prefer to hire help to build your off-the-grid home. You might want to garden, but you'll likely also use the grocery store and restaurants as you normally would. You'd probably prefer to keep your car and enjoy your community, but also escape endless utility bills and other drama.

Indeed, many people want to live off-the-grid to get away from the hectic pace of city living or to save money. Off-grid living can offer a kind of independence, peacefulness, and personal reward that is rarely found in our overly busy, technology-driven lives. Here's the "but"—and yes, I am afraid there is one and I'm not going to sugar coat it.

Buying remote land and building an off-grid home from scratch is not easy. It's still, to a large degree, the final frontier of modern real estate. This means there isn't a lot of precedent to rely on. It's absolutely not like building an on-grid home in the suburbs either. An off-grid home can be a real challenge and take several years to complete. I know there are many TV shows and videos on YouTube that make it look easy, but trust me, this will be one of the biggest self-imposed challenges you can undertake in today's world. Any author who says you can do this in a few years (or less) is one of the "do as I say, not as I've done," False Prophets I talked about earlier. Going off-the-grid is like getting an advanced degree in better and more independent living. It takes many years, a lot of patience, and lot of hard work. Obviously, the rewards are worth the trouble though.

As you will read in this book, I opted to leave city life for a remote—and, if I may say so, amazing—property in the wilds of Washington State. When I started researching my off-grid dream, I found it very hard to find good information about non-utility-based, rural home building. What I could find was often incomplete or barely readable. So, in conjunction with my off-grid evolution, I started writing this book. I hope this text will help you avoid many of the mistakes and missteps I made. I love living off-the-grid, and I'm excited to pass on what I know to other people interested in a more independent way of life. For all its challenges, this lifestyle more than makes up for it in tangible rewards—more on that soon.

What You'll Learn from This Book

The first of my Five Simple Life Principles is: *Knowledge is Power*. In this book I not only cover knowledge about what to do, but also about what you should never do while pursuing an off-grid lifestyle.

If you take away nothing else from this book, you should at least recognize the importance of pre-planning all aspects of your home before taking the leap of purchasing property or beginning to build. You must research everything thoroughly first! This includes the following topics, which form the backbone of this book.

PLANNING FOR A LIFESTYLE CHANGE: How can a person go from a 3000-square-foot (or more) home in the city to a small off-grid cottage in a remote area? It doesn't happen overnight. Chapters 1 through 3 will outline the mental and practical journey I made to do just that. If you're already weighed down by a lot of clutter,

I suggest you also grab my book *The Simple Life Guide to Decluttering Your Life.*

RESEARCHING AN OFF-THE-GRID HOME: All through this book, I will remind you of the importance of researching and planning before you build. I will stress the importance of building everything legally to code and explain how this critical step protects you, the homeowner. Building codes vary greatly throughout the country, and you need to safeguard your interests. Remember, Knowledge is Power. So don't skip this step!

CHOOSING AN OFF-THE-GRID PROPERTY: The property you buy will dictate how and what you can build, since you will be relying on that land for energy (whether solar, wind, micro-hydro, and/or geothermal), water (from a well or an aboveground), and waste management (via a septic system). Area topography and slope often dictate which of these systems will even work at a particular location.

Throughout this book I'll discuss why you shouldn't just blindly buy property and expect that your solar panels will get enough sun, or that your stream will provide enough drinking water, or that a building inspector will approve your septic permit. Thoughtful property selection is crucial to making it all work.

BUILDING AN OFF-THE-GRID HOUSE: This is where this book will save you a lot of headaches, and possibly tens of thousands of dollars in mistakes! I am going to give you plenty of knowledge on how to hire the best local contractors—and how to avoid the duds (who are plentiful, I'm sorry to say). We'll cover the pros and cons of DIY building versus hiring a pro. You'll learn about different kinds of off-grid construction and the tools you'll need to have on hand for most basic home repairs. Finally, you'll learn why I recommend building a small, regular home instead of a "tiny house", despite the trendiness of the tiny house movement.

OFF-THE-GRID CONNECTIVITY AND SECURITY: We'll discuss the best ways to ensure you have modern cell phone and internet connections while still being fully off-grid. You'll learn practical and afford-able ways to protect your property from would-be thieves, which sadly exist in remote locations just as they do in the city. We'll even discuss how to use wireless technology to monitor your off-grid home remotely, so you are always aware of what is happening at your property.

PAYING FOR YOUR OFF-THE-GRID PROJECT: When budgeting for an off-grid move, it's easy to make the mistake of accounting only for home and property costs, forgetting that it will cost serious money to build your water, waste, and energy systems too. These mistakes can cost you THOUSANDS of dollars and completely derail your entire project. Throughout this book, I will provide realistic price expectations for each off-grid component, and list companies and websites you can refer to that can help you budget for the different elements of your potential home.

Many would-be off-gridders forget to budget for costs that exist in remote areas but that are not normally associated with city liv-ing or buying a preexisting home. This includes building permits, tools, building inspections, gates and fences, creating or improv-ing roads, sheds, tree removal, well drilling, and an upgrade to a four-wheel drive vehicle or truck. This book will give you a clearer picture of all costs involved, so you can be realistic about your plans. Finally, I will share insider tips on how to finance an off-grid home, which is probably trickier than you realize.

Because of the above, and numerous people asking me about the cost of building off-grid; I wrote a book that walks you through the basics and process to come up with a starting budget: *The Beginners Guide To Living Off The Grid,* and a more advanced how-to online course found at (www.thesimplelifenow.com). The main thing I want this book to do is help you apply The Simple Life Principle #1: Knowledge is Power. As we unpack this knowledge, I'll introduce the other four Simple Life Principles and how they'll keep you on track and save you a ton of time and money during this adventure. Yes, I know I'm talking a lot about my other books. But remember, this is not a weekend seminar. We're talking about the biggest lifestyle change you'll ever make.

The Rewards of Off-The-Grid Living

If you're someone who wants more peace of mind, more sanity, and less clutter— you're going to LOVE living this lifestyle. But again, I'm not one to sugarcoat things. Living off-the-grid is not some kind of utopian paradise, no matter what the blogosphere tells you. Listen, if you go off-the-grid you will still need to pay your taxes and participate in the world. Things will still break and go wrong, and you will still have to deal with people who are incompetent and frustrating from time to time. You can't escape any of that completely.

However, the rewards of off-grid living are significant, and in my experience, absolutely worth it. You can save money, focus on what is authentic by simplifying your obligations, and live life on your own terms—isn't that the REAL American dream? This book was written to make the transition from a typical on-grid home to a modern comfortable off-grid home easier; and more achievable by applying the Five Simple Life Principles using practical solutions.

Whatever your reasons for streamlining your life, I wish you luck in your off-grid adventure. Having lived through that transition and all of its potential difficulties, I can say there is nowhere I'd rather be right now than in my remote home, enjoying a million-dollar lake view, listening to the sounds of nature, at peace with my place in the world. In putting this book out to the world, my wish is that it helps you, in some small way, to find the same peace.

How I Escaped "The Grid"

So where did the idea for my off-the-grid project come from? From one of those now popular living-in-the-wild Alaska shows? Or because of some misanthropic desire to completely detach myself from society and people? Neither. The answer is pretty simple actually: Because I wanted to. There were many factors, but I will begin my story by describing how I arrived at my decision to live off-the-grid.

First, I think it is important to understand that I grew up in a small town in the mountains of California, so what I'm doing is not as drastic as one might think. I did not go into this adventure completely in the dark. Also, this was not some off-the-cuff decision; there was a lot of thought and care that went into it. I feel it is important for people to see that even though I call it a *project*, it is ultimately a *life decision based upon finding my own personal freedom*.

If you're one of my readers who is living in the city and growing tired, or worried, about the relentless civil unrest in your streets, personal freedom is probably a big part of why you want to do this. City living has, honestly, never fully appealed to me. During my life I have lived in many cities across the country. As I have aged, I have become more disenchanted with and disengaged from city living. Not that it is a bad type of living; it's just not for me anymore.

Having grown up poor in a single-wide trailer, you would think I would not want to ever return to such a lifestyle. That couldn't be further from the truth. Having grown up that way has given me a different perspective on what I truly think is important.

Sure, at times things were tough growing up. I grew up sleeping in a bedroom where the ceiling leaked and it was cold enough to see my breath during the winter nights. I remember crawling under my blanket, head and all, to avoid freezing my ass off because we didn't have the money to buy a measly space heater. But these experiences made me appreciate everything I had that much more. They also made me more resourceful and self-reliant. I now look back and consider myself incredibly lucky to have grown up without a silver spoon up my butt. I was fortunate enough to know all the people in my town. When I waved at them, they would wave back. That is pretty much unheard of in a modern urban setting.

I still have fond memories of racing home from football practice, before the sun went down, to get in an hour of bird hunting. Heck, I would have my shotgun behind the seat of my truck to save time. Yes, that would mean I had a shotgun on school grounds, and I wasn't the only one. A lot of us did this, and no one busted into the school shooting people either. Most of us were hunters, and that was just all there was to it. Can you imagine what would happen to a kid doing that today?

Once I left my hometown for college at eighteen, I had very few opportunities to do the things I had so enjoyed while growing up hiking, fishing, hunting and just being in nature. For many years I yearned to return to that type of living. It is hard to explain to someone who has never experienced such a lifestyle, but for me this way of living has always made me the happiest.

To me, the daily grind of living in congested areas has become completely overwhelming and too stressful. Why would I want to sit in traffic if I don't have to? The thought of going to the mall actually makes me cringe. Why work hard at a job you (probably) don't even like, just to clutter your house up with stuff you don't really need? The fact that I didn't know any of my neighbors while living in the city was disturbing. I can't tell you how many people I waved at in my old neighborhood, while on my nightly walks, and received nothing but a strange look in return. Sometimes I got the middle finger salute (stupid teenagers).

On top of this, as I'm writing this second edition, entire sections of American cities are literally on fire due to civil unrest, and it's not because of some "greater good". So, on top of being harassed by noise, and traffic, and people in a big damn hurry, you also have to worry about an angry mob targeting your neighborhood, or the place you work. Is this really living? For me, I just don't think so. If you're still reading, I'm guessing you agree.

The thought of peace and tranquility today . . . well, most people consider it impossible to obtain. We've seemed to accept debt, clutter, traffic, noise and other drama as being normal. Back when I was still a member of the "Cult of Clutter", I believed these things as if they were inevitable. But as I started to become more and more frustrated with today's modern stresses, I began to think that there had to be a better way for those of us who desire a simpler and more balanced life.

How My Search Started

In late 2005, while living in Albuquerque, New Mexico (in a house too big for one guy and two dogs) I started longing more and more for simpler living. I started looking at remote properties in Colorado and New Mexico, but didn't make any serious decisions. In 2007, I went to work as a Special Agent for the FDA and moved back to California. I was working primarily in the Los Angeles area while living in San Diego. If you've ever made that trip (or even a piece of it), you can already guess what kind of daily stress I was under.

I began investigating if it was possible to obtain a place removed from the noise and the clutter of The Grid. I'll be honest, in the beginning it was pretty discouraging. Where do you start? Where is a good place to live? Could I handle a colder environment after living in sunny Southern California? Ah hell, I'll just put up with this crazy commute and 12-hour days for a few more years.

When I finally got serious, I started by going online and looking at properties in parts of the country I was interested in. I wanted to see what they cost and what the possibilities were for living in these places. During this time the housing boom was close to its peak and the land I was interested in was priced way too high. I knew, in time, the prices would have to come back down, so I put my dream on hiatus for a while.

After leaving the federal government in 2010, the thought was still in the back of my mind. The stress of trying to run my own business and numerous deaths, including one of my best friends, finally hit home. As such, I wasn't really pursuing my dream; I was just kind of in a rut. I knew, though, that if I kept saying "I will get to it next year," it would never happen and I would remain Gridlocked.

So with that, I rekindled my dream and put a plan into action. What followed was a long and challenging adventure, which I'll share as we move through the topics in this book. Those of you who have read my Simple Life Books know that I've made some mistakes along the way. While I'm not so naïve to think I can show you how to avoid your own mistakes, I know you will learn a lot from mine. You will save a lot of time, money, and drama by doing what this book advises you to do.

As I mentioned before, living off-the-grid doesn't mean living in a cave or shack with no running water or electricity. Today, that idea couldn't be further from the truth. Due to the improvements and affordability of alternative energy systems, you can now live a comfortable lifestyle on a piece of fairly isolated land. And in case you're worried about the cost of doing this, I can tell you that in the long run, it's much more reasonable.

I think that's the best part of this adventure. I'm doing it, financially, in a way that most Americans can afford. I do not come from a long line of millionaires. I do not have unlimited resources. My original mission was to complete the entire project—including land, well water, septic, dirt work/roads, and a small house—for a price that should be achievable for anyone with the desire to follow my path.

Hopefully you will enjoy your adventure, and even if you are not interested in such a lifestyle, maybe you will learn a little something that you can incorporate into your life to make it simpler and more enjoyable.

Going Off-The-Grid
IT STARTS WITH SIMPLIFYING YOUR LIFE

W hen you are thinking about living off-the-grid, or even contemplating starting a more self-sufficient lifestyle, I think you need a solid starting point. As I preach in my Simple Life Books—it is always better to have a plan and to take it slowly in the beginning. In fact, the second Simple Life Principle is *Avoid Extremes.* The trick is to take this one step at a time instead of expecting to go from being Grid-locked to living The Simple Life in ninety days, or even a full year.

Given the expectations of our instant gratification craving society, many people today forget that great things come with time, perseverance, and living with integrity. For example, my off-the-grid journey started around 2009, when I decided to downsize and simplify my life. After owning several homes that were much bigger than I needed, and filled with crap that I would never use, I decided it was time for a change. I had become a full-blown member of The Cult of Clutter! If you're living an over cluttered life right now, I'm guessing you can relate with how this happens.

Off-The-Grid Credo:
Stuff Doesn't = Happiness

U ntil I made the decision to go off-the-grid, I had spent my life being just what society wanted me to be: the ultimate consumer. I think it is no secret today that our lives are plagued by the long work days, exhausting work weeks so we can make enough money to buy products that will (hopefully) fill the void that is unhappiness in our life. Now, I'm not putting down hard work. I worked damn hard to get where I am today. I also don't begrudge any of the time I spent working hard and earning an honest wage. But, I do think we have our priorities way out of whack when it comes to how we spend the money we worked so hard to earn.

Why do we buy the biggest house we can get a loan for? Why do we buy that sports car we really can't afford? Why do we have a closet full of clothes and shoes we hardly wear? In the end, we stress ourselves out so we can have all these things, and for what? More importantly, why have so many young people run directly off the cliff of consumerism and are now demanding the lackeys in DC to rescue them with a bunch of bloated government programs? Exactly! You can't answer that question because there is no logical or reasonable answer, except we have given up our personal freedoms for the dopamine hit of acquiring shiny objects we do not need and cannot afford. All to keep the machinery of greed and corruption running on rocket fuel . . . *our* rocket fuel!

To me the answer is simple. We do all these things, and drive ourselves crazy in the process, because we've been told that this is how we find happiness. According to the dogma of The Grid, stuff equals happiness. Trust me, I followed this mantra with gusto, buying all kinds of junk I didn't need. I was a multiple credit card carrying member of the Cult of Clutter.

Stop Being a Crap Collector

So where do you start your journey to simpler living? Well, just like an addict, you start by admitting you have a problem. I like to give the moniker "Crap Collector" or "Clutter Clinger" to the affliction most of us suffer from today. As humans, it seems like our primary goal in life is to compile as much useless stuff as we can. Just so we can die among our heaps of our non-gloriously obtained items, hoping someone finds us before one of our pets starts eating our face! Ok, I know that is a little over the top, but we need to understand just how nuts this "widget in, widget out" lifestyle is. We work to make widgets, so we can earn money to buy more widgets, so someone else can make money to buy their own widgets.

Just as I said above, the starting point is realizing that your life is worth more than this. You were meant for more than just surrounding yourself with shiny widgets. The appeal of a new widget only lasts for a while, and then you have to buy more, and more, and more.

This is why I realized that having less is the secret to LIVING a life of more. Living The Simple Life off-the-grid will be a little different for everyone. For some, it will mean building their own dwelling by hand, having no running water, and growing or raising all of their own food. For others it might mean buying a smaller house and installing some solar panels. Others might want to be somewhere in the middle.

As for me, I wanted to live in a comfortable, up-to-date home, but downsize and simplify my life in terms of both financial obligations and "stuff" ownership. In other words, less junk, fewer headaches, and more time for what truly matters in life—all without giving up the comforts of the modern world. Does that sound good to you?

So, the starting point for me was to greatly downsize my living space. Back then, I was paying a ridiculous mortgage for a 1,700-square-foot house in Southern California, and constantly losing sleep trying to figure out how I would pay for it. Sound familiar?

What's even crazier is that I was single and had two dogs. Why I thought I needed that much space is a mystery to me even today. Well, not really; I was brainwashed into thinking bigger was better. I had been duped by the dogma of The Grid.

In the end, all that extra stuff and space just stressed me out, financially and emotionally. Not to mention the heaps of time and money spent on upkeep for that huge house and property. I could have been using that time doing something I truly enjoyed. If this sounds familiar, believe me, you're not alone.

That is one important point I want to make about living in the Cult of Clutter: Instead of making us happy, in the end it actually makes us less happy. It takes time away from those we care about and from pursuing our passions and living our purpose.

We spend a great deal of our lives pursuing the things that we have been told will make us happy, but in the end, they make us miserable and unfulfilled. If that isn't true irony, I don't know what is. Wow, the joke is on us.

The great news is that you can change this just as I did. That's why I want to share with you my experience and the steps you can take in order to "happify" (my made-up word) and simplify your life! Decluttering your life is the first step toward going off-the-grid.

The American Dream, or the American Nightmare?

When planning to go off-the-grid, the first thing you need to analyze are your current living conditions. Can you get by with less living space? I would say almost everyone in this country could answer this with a resounding *yes*! My first step toward going off-the-grid was simple; I analyzed my monthly living expenses. This included my mortgage, insurance, utilities, and general upkeep expenses. It came out to an astounding $3,500 a month. Remember, this is for a single person with two dogs. Also remember this was in 2009. Today, these expenses are even higher for the average American.

For those of you who do not live in California, or one of the more expensive states, you are probably flabbergasted by that number. Let me tell you, that is cheap in Southern California. Most people I know in California easily spend around $5,000 to $6,000 per month or more for what I outlined above. Matter of fact, I have middle-class friends in California spending $8,000 to $9,000 a month . . . wow! When I look back with my "what is important to me" clarity I see these monthly expenses as nuts. Once you make this transition, you'll probably feel the same way.

Before making my big move, I still had about 27 years left on my mortgage. So I could look forward to spending a total of $1,134,000 (yes, that is over a million dollars) if I maintained that lifestyle. Here is the kicker; most of us don't maintain our current expenses. We upgrade! So, if I hadn't escaped The Grid when I did, that $1 million plus figure would have been higher!

Basically, we all have the capability to be millionaires (matter of fact I prove this with basic math in by book *The Simple Life Guide to Financial Freedom*). All we have to do is adjust our lifestyles choices. That is a pretty astounding statement. Just thinking of the average person I know in California—their total expenses (monthly and long-term) would be close to double or triple mine. I hope you are starting to see the insanity of the consumer-based economy of The Grid.

Some readers might consider this lifestyle change rather drastic. But I will assure you once I got settled in my new, downsized place (described below) it was anything but. It was a huge relief. As I outlined, I was living in the typical Southern California residential neighborhood in a three-bedroom, two bath, two-car garage house. For a single guy, this is just way too much space. Heck, I think it is too big for the average family, and I will explain why later.

Is Renting a Sensible Option?

After analyzing how much my house cost each month, I decided to take a look at renting and see what made sense. The first place I looked at was on Craigslist.com. It was very discouraging in the beginning, as renting in California is fairly expensive when compared to the rest of the country. Not to mention, I was looking just after the housing bubble had burst between 2008 and 2009 (the start of the Great Recession), so everyone was trying to do what I was doing, and the glut of prospective renters was pushing rents even higher.

The icing on the cake was having two large dogs. Most rental owners really don't like pets. When they do accept them, they almost always hit you with a significant upcharge. So what did that mean? Instead of renting in my general location, I had to cast a wider net to find more options. Having pets meant I had to look in more rural areas, where people didn't really care as much about renting to pet owners.

At first, I started by looking for two-bedroom places. I quickly realized that the price difference between what I was currently paying and the prospective rental was not large enough to justify the move. This forced me to really start looking outside my comfort zone. I started looking at studios, granny flats (small apartments attached to houses) and cottages (basically a studio house—all living space is in one area as with a studio apartment). That was in 2010. It was my first step towards living The Simple Life.

This opened up an entire new lifestyle that I had never experienced before. It simplified living far more than what I was used to. It is amazing how having less space forces you to have less stuff, which ultimately makes you happier. Huh, I'll be honest, I really didn't see that happening in the beginning of my search. That is how brainwashed I had become—pretty amazing when you consider we come from hunter-gathers who carried all their belongings on their back!

I'm sharing this story to show you that I know how hard downsizing can be. Sometimes you might get lucky and find the place you want right away. But, from my experience, making such a drastic change takes time, because:

- You'll most likely end up living in a different kind of habitation than you ever have before.
- You will probably have to search in new, unfamiliar areas to determine what works best for your current situation.

Here is the key: Change is always painful in the beginning. In spite of what other self-help authors say, there is no getting around this. You have to realize you are making a major life shift. It is going to be uncomfortable. All great things in life come with some scrapes and bruises along the way.

My search for a rental home in Southern California took six months. I did a lot of research and soul-searching during this period, and ultimately, it paid off. I found a cottage with a full-sized yard in a rural part of San Diego.

It ended up being the nicest place I had found and with the lowest rent (several hundred dollars a month lower!). The surprise was that my landlords were the best I have ever had. When you take your time and are patient, a little luck will come your way.

I will emphasize that when renting you really need to evaluate whom you are renting from, just as they are evaluating you. For most, moving is not a pleasant experience, so my philosophy is not to do it more than you have to! When I moved into my new-to-me rental in San Diego, I knew I would be there for at least two years.

That is another key to think about. How long do you plan to live in this place? Can you stay long term if need be? If you own, will you be able to sell your house in a timely manner, or will you have to try and turn it into a rental?

In my situation I was unsure how long I would be there. That's why I made sure it was something I could do long term if I needed to. Thankfully, I thought that through because I ended up being in the cottage rental far longer than I had originally expected, four years instead of two.

I know most of you who are married and have children are going . . .

"Yeah, that's not a problem for a single guy, but our situation is different."

Yes and no. I know families who have reduced their living area by half with no problem at all. I also know families who sold all their belongings and who now travel around the country in an RV. Sure, at first they and their kids had to get used to the new lifestyle. But once they adapted, I have not heard one complaint about not having enough space. Again, it is about facing the challenge and not giving in to the voice that says, "It is just too hard."

Now, after spending several years around remote and nomadic living people, I can tell you this with 100 percent certainty—single people are the anomaly in these types of lifestyles. This surprises most who give me the "you're single, I can't do that" excuse: Most people living the off-the-grid and nomadic lifestyle (such as RV living) are married or couples, with kids, and pets for that matter.

Simplifying your life comes with challenges, and you have to keep your eyes on the prize at the end. More financial stability ultimately means more freedom. I'm not saying that minimizing your living space and having more disposable income is the solution to all your problems. But I can promise you this; it is easier to figure all this out when you don't have piles of monthly expenses to worry about.

How My Patience Finally Paid Off

The 2008 recession was not kind to most of us. I'll be honest, back in 2010, just before I moved into my first rental, I ended up selling my house for a significant loss to the tune of a few hundred thousand dollars.

But I had to make a critical choice. I could either let the house push me into bankruptcy or I could make a short-term loss for long-term happiness. These were incredibly tough circumstances, but I don't regret choosing happiness for a second. By forcing myself way out of my comfort zone, I found a great rental place for a great price. That was my big payoff. Less financial worries gave me more mental bandwidth to focus on the next stage of my adventure.

Now, I know you are asking "So, how big was the cottage?" My new rental place was around 475 square feet (based on my measurements). That is right, I went from 1,700 to 475 square feet, almost a 75 percent reduction in living space!

Do I recommend everyone make such a drastic change? Of course not. Again, it depends on your situation and what you are comfortable with. I will tell you this, I have no regrets and the thought of ever again living in a big house never crossed my mind. Not to mention, I have since met numerous people who have done the same. We all agree that it was one of the best decisions we have ever made. I think you'll agree once you take this first step yourself.

Now let's get down to the nitty gritty—how much money did I save and what difference did it make? I was able to go down from $3,500 in basic living expenses per month, to $1,100 a month. The best part for me was not only saving a lot of money, but also not having all the stress of paying for and maintaining a large house. That payoff was priceless. Most people underestimate how much mental and emotional energy they're wasting just trying to maintain all their material excess. You'll realize this difference yourself the moment you downsize your life. You'll be amazed

Another bonus was that I had to sell a lot of stuff, because there was no way it was going to fit into the rental cottage. I made close to $10,000 selling all my extra crap on Craigslist. And I sold most of it in just 48 hours! I can't explain the cleansing effect this had on my psyche and life. After selling all those useless possessions it felt as if a huge weight had been lifted off my shoulders.

This was my real-life experience in taking the first step into The Simple Life. As most of you know from my other books, products, teachings, and writings, I never give advice about things unless I've done them myself.

Bottom line, I learned that home ownership not only costs you financially, but can put you in a situation where you're Gridlocked and unable to even see a way out of the chaos. Again, that all changes the moment you start downsizing. Case in point, I used my time in the rental place to plot out my next move (which turned out to be this off-the-grid project!) and to make sure I would not be rushing into anything. I know not everything can be planned, nor do our plans always work out perfectly. But I like to give myself the best odds possible to avoid as many pitfalls as I can.

I can now say that my patience has paid off big time. Today, I have the property of my dreams. It's still going to be a lot of hard work, but I wouldn't have it any other way. I now have the time and energy to pursue my true life's purpose and to be happy in the present. That's the final point I want to make about living off-the-grid; if you are bored, you are doing it wrong. While living off-grid there is always a project that needs to be done—real life is about constant motion and improvement. Matter of fact, I have a saying . . .

"Action is the pudding of life, why would you not want to make and eat more pudding!"

This means that the ultimate goal of going off-the-grid is to discover your life's purpose and start working on it. But first, let's talk about where you'll be living.

First Things First
HOW TO FIND YOUR OFF-THE-GRID PROPERTY

Since I started my "Off-The-Grid Project" many people have asked me how I found my ideal property. Those who have seen it have even noted that the land and view look amazing, and I'd like to humbly agree. But as to the question of how I actually found it . . . well, that's not an easy question to answer.

It didn't happen overnight, and there is no magic formula for finding a great place to live off-the-grid. As I have discussed previously, my property is unique to my wants and desires, and yours should be specific to your own goals as well.

With that being said, I think I have come up with a decent method for locating and evaluating potential properties that will work for most. If you are looking for an *easy* formula for finding the perfect off-the-grid spot, I will warn you: There is no easy way. It will take time and a great deal of work. Having said that, I hope you'll find my story and strategies useful.

How I Hatched My Plan

My plan to finally make my dream a reality was originally devised while I was living in New Mexico (around 2005) during my employment with the federal government. Anyone who has been to New Mexico knows there are numerous outdoor activities in the area in which a sports-inclined person may participate. In that way, New Mexico brought back memories of my childhood growing up in a small town in the Sierra Nevada Mountain Range.

By that point in my career, I had been fortunate enough to have done a great deal of traveling while working in the government. Because of this broad geographic exposure, I already had a few places I was looking at in terms of buying my ideal off-the-grid land.

Washington State was at the top of my list for three reasons:

1. I love the outdoors, and Washington State has tons to offer in this area.

2. Affordability: When I compared land prices in other states, such as Idaho, Montana, and Wyoming, Washington definitely offered the most bang for my buck.

3. Washington has no state income tax. I'm not a big fan of giving the government any more money than I need to.

I had a friend who lived in Northwest Washington, and I used to go visit him once or twice a year. He lived in a fairly congested part of the state. I knew I wanted something more remote, but I just wasn't sure where. As luck would have it, after a transfer for my federal government job back to Southern California, I was assigned to assist on a case in the Spokane area in the northeastern part of Washington State.

While working there, I also met a girl, and we dated for a while. So I was able to explore that part of Washington a bit more, and it was love at first sight (with the area—not the girl, unfortunately).

Now, it was some four years after I had my original idea to eventually live off-the-grid. I had contacted a real estate agent when the idea had hit me living in New Mexico years earlier. However, my first blush of enthusiasm quickly dampened because land prices were out of my range due to the pre-recession housing boom being in full effect. But I didn't give up. I knew the prices would eventually come back to Earth. And of course, they soon did.

Why Patience is the Key

There is one thing I can't emphasize enough when it comes to starting your going off-the-grid adventure patience, patience, and some more patience. Again, there is no roadmap for this type of life. Everyone takes their own path and finds what they are looking for via different avenues.

The part of Washington in which I finally found my own personal paradise is littered with people who had once aspired to a rural and self-sufficient life. But, they didn't do their research first, jumped in too quickly, and flamed out. Every time I mentioned I was from Southern California and described what I was trying to do, a local would give me the look like . . .

"Yeah, right buddy. You will be gone in less than a year, if even that long."

Honestly, I can't blame them, as most people today jump into things without thinking it through.

Unfortunately, there are plenty of authors who are eager to tell these people exactly what they want to hear. In my Simple Life Books, I call these authors the "False Prophets". False Prophets are in the self-help world and have been slowly creeping into the off-the-grid world. Some of them have tried to rip me off. You'll find their books on Amazon. These authors either rip off someone else's ideas or tell you what you want to hear because that's the only way they can sell their books.

What does this have to do with you finding your ideal rural land, you might ask? First, it's important to be careful about who you listen to. Again, I never teach anything in my books that I haven't done myself. That said, here's my hard-won advice.

First, you have to be dedicated to the idea of changing your lifestyle, and it should be with real intention and thought, and not just something you're curious about.

Second, when you arrive at your new destination, don't try to change the community to be like the place you just left. Californians are famous for this. Just ask natives of Texas and Colorado. They're watching floods of Californians come to their state trying to escape the high income taxes and other crap that they voted for in the first place. Then, they come to Texas and Colorado, and other places and create the same kinds of problems. Don't be one of these people. If you are moving to a new area, you need to adapt to it, not demand that everyone adapt to you.

Third, by hailing from outside the area in which you intend to build, you will have an uphill climb ahead of you just to gain the trust and respect of the locals. I will expand on this statement a little later, but it is incredibly important. Just remember, you are not the first one to come up with this remote-living idea. Many wannabe off-gridders have made it harder for people like you and I to move to remote areas and be welcomed warmly by the locals.

Coming Up with Your Own Rational Plan

If you think you may want to head off-the-grid for a simpler and more self-sufficient life, I recommend you start by asking yourself . . .

"Why do I want this type of lifestyle?"

Do you want it because it looks cool on TV? (I do not recommend this as a valid reason!)

Do you just want a simpler life? Do you want a remote vacation house to get away from it all?

Everyone will have their own motivations, but this suggestion about soul-searching has a concrete point. Moving away from urban areas must be something you truly want to do and a lifestyle you really want to adopt.

There are many variations of what "living a more remote lifestyle" looks like in practice. No matter what your preferences, the process of finding your off-the-grid land will be relatively the same as mine, or anyone else's. The only thing that will be different is how remote your piece of property will be.

For me, the best way to start was by traveling to various parts of the United States to see what places I liked most. I needed to come up with a short list of potential locations. I have been fortunate and have spent a great deal of time traveling for my job. But for many people, this is not possible. If you have no idea where to start, I suggest looking on the internet for states or areas that have what is on your wish list (climate, land features, state taxes, laws, and so on).

Once you have five to ten locations in mind, search the internet for land for sale in those places. This will give you an idea of the size of the lots that are available, and what the price range for real estate generally is in that area. When I first started, I used *www.zillow.com* and *www.realtor.com*, as most types of properties for sale were listed on these sites. Today, I would recommend www.zillow.com as www.realtor.com just isn't the same as it was. Of course, don't rely exclusively on this type of search. This is just to give you an idea if what you are looking for is affordable and/or available.

After narrowing your locations down, the hard work begins. I would keep your list simple, like five states (or areas) or fewer. Just like anything in life, you have to experience an area first hand in order to figure out if it is the right thing for you. Remember the Simple Life Principle #1, *Knowledge is Power*—and first-hand experience is the best kind of knowledge. For me, I planned my vacations in the areas I was interested in moving to so that I could experience them up close and in person.

My Embarrassing Life Lesson in Realtor Shopping

Now, don't make the mistake I made and go with the first "remote property specialist" who you contact. That mistake almost ended my entire off-the-grid project. One day, while surfing the internet looking for properties in Northeast Washington I saw an ad for a specialist on remote real estate. I called the number and talked to a guy who told me everything I wanted to hear.

"Yeah, I know plenty of great properties within your price range. They're exactly what you're looking for, Gary!"

So far, so good. Sort of. I walked into their Spokane real estate office on a weekend, to meet with the agent I had spoken to on the phone. He walked out of the back like he'd just crawled out of a dumpster. Bald, crumpled clothes, looking like an Aryan Nation guy who was in the midst of sleeping off a 72-hour vodka marathon. As someone who shows up to business meetings in jeans and flip flops, I didn't get alarmed over this. But I was already a little uneasy. He pulled a list of properties, printed it up, and we arranged to set up an official time to take a ride and check them out. I was staying at a hotel in a small town about 40 miles north. He showed up in a car that should have long been put out of its misery. We're talking about a banged up, rust ridden old Subaru that looked like he'd driven it off the junk yard lot the night before. I almost backed out as the first alarm bell went off in my head, but I'd come a long way. Then, things got weirder . . .

"Hey, do you mind driving . . ."

"Um, yeah, I do mind."

Ugh, what was with this guy? I was in a Ford Mustang rental. The rental place was out of 4-Wheel drives.

"Okay, we can use my car. But it's really dirty."

Another alarm going off in my head saying "nope, call this day off," but, I got in the car. After all, he said he "knew the area". That turned out to be horseshit. We got lost twice. I'm not talking about a few wrong turns either. These were journeys far past the borders of "the middle of nowhere". About ninety minutes into my road trip with Captain Dipshit, his car started to overheat. When we popped the hood, the radiator cap was missing.

"Dude, your radiator cap is gone."

"Oh, yeah, is that bad?"

My day was just getting better and better. We screwed the cap back on, that I luckily found lying on a flat bracket below the radiator. On we went, and made it a couple more miles before the car started to putter and snort like a dying water buffalo. It was hot as Satan's Sauna outside, and I had no idea where we were. Next step, we found a pinhole in his radiator.

"Dude, there's a hole in your radiator."

"Oh, yeah, guess that's pretty bad too, right?"

Holy shit, how does this guy get his pants on in the morning?

We stopped at some rusted out 7-11 and bought easy radiator sealant. That got us to the first "property", where an overbuilt, redneck rigged "house" sat in the middle of what looked like an amateur junk yard. What a shithole. I was getting pissed off and embarrassed at the same time. A couple more shithole properties and I decided to abort the road trip . . .

"Hey, it's getting late and I'm worried about being stuck out in the middle of nowhere with your car the way it is."

We headed back. Of course, his car sputtered and stalled as we were going 70 miles per hour on the highway. Big surprise there. We pulled over, again. We popped the hood, again.

"Oh, you know I might be out of gas."

"NO, the fuel gauge is still at half."

"Yeah, but my fuel gauge is broken. I don't know . . . but I put like $5 in before I came here."

He gets under the car to take a look.

"I think I smell gas," I said, taking a look now myself.

"Yeah, me too."

"Uh, your fuel line is loose."

As a former investigator, my first thought was . . . fuel lines and radiator caps, just don't come lose at the same time!

"Hey, I think someone might have done this to your fuel line."

"Oh yeah, me and my neighbors don't get along well!"

Ever had one of those moments when you wondered if you were on hidden camera? This was one of those moments for me. After clamping his fuel line Donald Duck style, he pulls out a scratched-up cell phone and calls his father-in-law. Turned out, the father-in-law owned the real estate office where this dipshit of humanity worked.

Good God, this guy only has a job because some poor guy didn't want his daughter to starve to death on Skid Row.

While we were waiting for his father-in-law, he wanders off into the tree line and leaves me in the road.

"Hey, if you want your father-in-law to see us, we should be where he can see us."

"Yeah, I gotta keep out of sight though. So, if the cops come, could you, like, talk to them? Just tell them what we're doing."

"Why?"

"Because I might have had some run-ins with cops."

"What!?"

"Like. I mean, I might have resisted arrest."

It was ninety degrees outside. We were out of water. Thank God I had a knife on me, and my law enforcement training. Sometimes, you've gotta just look on the bright side. His father-in-law showed up. That was my last date with my first "Remote Property Specialist". He "Cable Guyed" me for a few weeks after, with voice mails like . . .

"Hey man, I've got some properties you're gonna like! I'll shoot ya' the list and let's meet."

Ever the optimist, I did visit a few more properties on his list. Most were garbage lots, that I couldn't put a travel trailer on much less a house. My favorite was literally on the side of the mountain. There was no plateau. It would cost at least $100k of dirt work just to get a road to the house. I would also have to remove a lot of trees and I could already see my poor dog, Barnie, rolling down the slope of the mountain every time I opened the door to let him out for his morning potty break. Some of the mosquitoes were carrying harpoons and seemed to be wearing military grade body armor. It was a mile long, ankle-twisting hike up to the lot from the end of the "road".

I drove my trusty rental Mustang and beat it to shit getting up to the walking point. I got a rock the size of a football stuck between the brake disc and the disc protection plate. It took me doing a Secret Service style J turn (you see those in high-speed James Bond style car chases) to jolt the rock lose. I was so disenchanted and pissed off, I almost took this as a sign that my off-grid adventure was not meant to be.

Thankfully, I still had my real estate license otherwise I probably would have bought one of these horrible properties not knowing any better. After recovering from this drama, I decided to head to the local bank to see if they had repossessions available. That turned out to be a good move, as I'll explain later. But I share this embarrassing story to show you how quickly things can go off the rails if you try to shortcut any of the steps in this book. Eventually I figured this out.

The right way looks like this: Do all your research before even talking to a Realtor. This way, you know exactly what you're looking for. After dealing with the "King of The Village Idiots", I started over and researched what type of land I needed for the type of home I wanted. Only then did I find a real estate agent local to the area. If you try to use a real estate agent too early in the process, you will waste a lot of time looking at land *they* want you to buy. For example, I bought a second property (in the beginning of 2020) in another state, and have been looking at remote properties in other locations for the last ten years while completing my first off-the-grid home. You would think it would be easy by now, but I still run into the clueless realtor problem. You might also end up stranded in the middle of nowhere with someone as loveable as my first would-be realtor. There's an unsettling thought.

After wasting days on dumpy and unbuildable lots, I learned my lesson. I realized I needed to do my own homework first, rather than relying on the real estate agent to do it for me. As you now see, this can be a really bad idea.

Also, keep in mind that some remote lots are not listed, as they are "for sale by owner" only. Your local real estate agent has a better chance of knowing about these lots. People local to the area might know of someone trying to sell some unlisted land. This is where you'll find those sweet deals that no one else knows about. Again, a non-local realtor won't know any of these things.

How I Redeemed Myself and Found My Dream Property

After wasting time with multiple "Joe City Slicker" Realtors, I decided to spend three to four days traversing the area I was interested in by car. Take my advice: This is the best way to figure out if that region suits your needs, hands down. I put about

1,000 miles on my rental car in three days. But I'll tell you what, I learned where I wanted to live, and more specifically, what I was looking for by doing this.

Once I had narrowed down my search to a specific place, I was ready to find a good *local* real estate agent. During this time, I had been getting to know the locals in the town in which I was staying. I asked everyone I could about land. I asked if they knew anyone who had property for sale. This approach didn't get me any new leads on lots for sale, but it eventually led me to the right person to get the ball rolling.

After asking around, someone told me I should go to the local bank and see if they had any foreclosed or short sale properties for sale. Now, this was an excellent idea! So, with my newfound enthusiasm, I headed off to the local bank. I ended up speaking with the vice president of the branch and asked if she had any land for sale. She didn't, but she said she knew a Realtor at one of the local real estate offices who specialized in the type of land I was looking for. Even better, the person selling the land resided in the same area in which I was considering buying.

It was pretty funny. I didn't even have to get in my car to go to the real estate office. I literally walked two blocks from the bank, and I was there. After introducing myself to the Realtor and outlining my master plan, he told me he knew of a property that was exactly what I was looking for. Of course, I was a little skeptical because the last real estate agent had said exactly the same thing. But after he brought up the listing on his computer and showed it to me, I was inclined to think that he just might be right. In addition, he found another property near the first one which he thought might work too. He got it!

So, my new Realtor and I made a plan to meet early the next morning and head out to take a look at the properties. The next morning, I met up with my new real estate agent, and we went to see a 20-acre secluded lot with a view of a nearby lake (water nearby was one of my absolute requirements).

After weaving through an old logging road for about 45 minutes, we arrived at the property. It was land still owned by the logging company that had worked the area years back. I mention this because early on I had been discouraged from looking at these types of lots. That turned out to be a huge mistake.

For example, my first real estate agent—way back in New Mexico—wouldn't give me logged lots to look at. His rational was that such spots had been "stripped bare of trees". His opinion was that, for someone like me, (who wanted to live in the forest) a lack of trees wouldn't make much sense.

This may seem to be logical at first glance, but here's why the opposite is actually true. . . .

While some logging lots have been stripped bare, this is not true for all of them. Especially if there were smart lumberjacks on the job. The logging company from which I bought my lot had a business model based on *reselling* land. They selectively cut trees, which keeps the forest in a condition ideal for someone who wants to develop the land or make a homestead. Pretty smart I would say. A savvy logging company can make money off the trees, and then make money selling the lots. Now that you know this, don't let anyone fool you with this "all the trees will be gone" nonsense, because it's just not the case.

The logging company that owned my would-be lot had left me plenty of trees, as it turns out. True, they cleared most, but not all the good ones. They left trees that were not profitable for them to cut, but they were great for someone like me, who was looking to build a house in the woods and live on the property.

But here is the real genius in their lot-reselling plan. A logging company has to build a "landing" at its worksites. A landing is the spot where all the heavy logging equipment is placed and the trees are de-branched, de-barked, and prepared for transport. The company that had worked my land had cleverly built the "landing" in the best building site for a future house.

This was great for me! I would have far less work to do, and much less dirt to move, in order to make my lot house-ready. By selectively clearing the trees, instead of seeming like a barren scar, the property was made appealing to me as a buyer.

Most people who looked at the lot before me couldn't see the potential, because most real estate agents don't have a clue how to develop such a property. But my new local real estate agent got it!

We walked the property and saw all the potential, and how much of the hard work had already been done.

Here's a summary of what we saw:

- The building site was already established in the best location and was flattened and settled. It would take minimal work to finish. This is especially important when dealing with sloped land, like on a mountainside.
- Because the trees had been selectively cleared already, I wouldn't have to remove literally hundreds of trees to make the property buildable.
- Substantial amounts of work had already been done by the logging company in building roads that granted access to the site.

It's hard to overstate how valuable these three things were to me as the property buyer. Tallying up the combination of earth-moving and tree removal, I probably saved around $100,000 and weeks, if not months, of extra labor. Of course, if you purchase a lot that has a large number of trees, you can always work out a deal with a local logger to harvest some of your trees. When done correctly, you will benefit from the trees being cleared and you'll make some money on the timber. I know this firsthand, as I have purchased another 30 acres since I wrote the first edition of this book and done just that. Now, that is a win, win! And here's one more important point that most potential buyers saw as a negative but was actually another big positive. . . .

The lower portion of my property had transport power lines running through it. Now these weren't the type of power lines I could tap into for electricity, but the industrial-grade kind that transport high voltage electricity to other parts of the state. Most people would look at these and think *"no way!"* But that would be a big mistake.

First, these power lines were far enough away from the living area to be of no concern. You can't even see them from most of the property. Second, the power company had to maintain the road used to service these wires. This service road runs through the lower part of my property as an access road. The other power company road leads almost all the way to my upper building area . . . that complimentary, ongoing road maintenance is a big-time bonus!

This is a critical point. If you have only lived in a city, you have probably only driven on public roads, maintained over the years by local or state governments. You may not even have heard of private roads. But in many rural areas, roads are private, meaning the people living on them must pay for and arrange for their maintenance. Building, and especially paving, a road is expensive. Also, don't forget maintenance such as fixing the inevitable potholes, cracks, and erosion that appear over time. If you've ever driven off road and been stuck in the mud, or damaged your vehicle, you know what I'm talking about. So having these drive-ready roads is a HUGE plus. Also, you would in theory have to share the road maintenance cost equally with all your neighbors. Imagine having to arrange that kind of deal and get everyone paying their part on time. Good luck with that.

So I was doubly thrilled that by the time I had bought the land and come back to begin building my home, the power company had completely re-done the road and done a great job! This left me with only about 200 yards of road that I needed to fix. That saved me probably another $20,000 and years of work. Just imagine having no road to reach your house and having to pay to have the entire thing paved or rocked yourself. Better yet, think about that road in your city that it took the government years to finish building. How would you like to manage a smaller version of that project as the first part of your off-the-grid adventure? No thanks.

The Benefit of Being Flexible About Your Property

I know what you are thinking . . .

> *"Gary this all sounds great, but how much did this amazing piece of property cost you?"*

Ah, that's the best part. It was a great price because no one had seen through all the supposed negatives. I bought 20 acres of gorgeous mountain land for $23,000. No, there is not a misplaced comma—that is twenty-three thousand dollars. That is far less than what most people pay for their yuppie, "I'm-really-cool, competing-with-the-Jones" sports car that they really can't afford.

And guess what? I just did almost the same thing in 2020. I bought 20 acres in another state for $25,000. The original owners paid $100,000! There are deals to be had, you just have to put in the time and effort.

As I've said before, a little luck helps in the process, but I wouldn't plan on getting lucky. I had already planned on how to deal with the road issue, but fortunately I didn't have to. That was my lucky break. But I had a plan going into it, and so should you.

You can see that by being patient and doing research, I made something that seemed impossible a reality. I hope my story saves you from wasting time and effort (as I did) while finding your dream land.

So, remember, patience is the most important quality and research is the most critical activity when searching for your off-grid land. Be sure you can commit time, energy, and resources to your project over several years. Create a wish-list of what you are looking for in terms of weather, topography, state laws, local culture, etc. Remember, your land will dictate which alternative energy systems and home building techniques you can use. Make sure to create a wish-list of home and system features you want. You're more likely to find them if you do!

While virtual research (via the internet) is good, use this only to narrow down your options. Consider vacationing in the place you wish to live. This way, you can ensure it's right for you. Do all of this before contacting a local Realtor. This kind of homework will save you lots of time and money.

Your Water Supply

THE DIFFERENCE BETWEEN LIVING OFF-THE-GRID AND "PERMANENT CAMPING"

Remember those back-yard camping trips from when you were a kid? You'd pitch a tent out back, grab some blankets, some bug spray, a jug of water and a couple granola bars. If you ran out of water, no problem! You'd just go back to the house and grab some water, or a coke. Not so when you're living off-the-grid. Water is the easiest thing to take for granted . . . until you don't have it. If I had to pick one thing that most people don't fully consider when going off-the-grid, this is it.

If you want to live off-the-grid in a more remote location, your first and biggest problem will be how to access water. As basic as this seems, you would be surprised how many people ignore this simple, yet necessary component in the off-the-grid/remote living lifestyle. Matter of fact, when it comes to the one thing most people fail to think about—it is access to water. A close second is coming up with a budget for the project (more on that later). We are so used to turning on the faucet and getting instant water that we forget how precious it is to be connected to the public utility system.

When I started looking for my land several years back, the first thing I would always focus on was access to water. You can get water from several sources, such as a creek, river, pond, or (most frequently) from a well. It is always nice to have a natural water source on your property, but this is not usually the case. It's more than likely that you will drill a standard well to get the faucets going. Wells will be a major focus in this chapter.

The bottom line is that without a reliable water source on your property, you have nothing but an expensive camping site. The key word here is *reliable*. I know people who regularly haul water to their property in trucks because they don't have *reliable* access to water. Some people have no water access at all. To me, becoming a frequent water bearer is more work than it is worth. It's smarter to focus on buying a property that can provide a reliable source of water. This way you don't have to manage an unreliable, expensive, and time-consuming system of carrying water to your land. Not to mention, if you live in an area that gets a lot of snow during the winter—good luck hauling it up bad roads. It might be pretty much impossible when those bad roads are frozen!

When it comes to reliable water, having a well is the smartest thing you can do—even if you live on a property that has its own water source. Due to the extreme droughts throughout the United States and especially in the West, wells are becoming increasingly popular. Of course, due to supply and demand, that also means that well-drilling services are skyrocketing. So, it may be a while before you can get a company out to your property to do the job.

When I got my well drilled, there was high demand for drilling professionals because of the droughts in the West. Even people with only an acre were trying to drill their own wells. So, dozens of brand-new drilling companies started popping up. I caught this at just the right time, and the guy who managed my well-drilling project actually became a friend. Turned out, he was preparing to retire from a long and successful career in the industry, and just happened to pick up the phone when I called. Guess I deserved some good karma after that little road trip with my first Realtor. Before that, I called on a Witcher who used dowsing to find my best spot for water. If I remember right, we used the exact witching spot to start our drilling project.

If this sounds "out there" to you, keep in mind that it's dumber to just go with the first drilling professional you find. Some are too lazy to do the job right, others lack integrity, and many are a horrid combination of both. Some of them will gladly take your money and completely rip you off when it comes time to deliver the service. That is the nature of the beast: once a somewhat pricey service becomes popular, the dishonest crooks come out of the woodwork to cash in. So be careful when hiring a drilling company.

Of course, there are also properties for sale that have a well already drilled and a pump installed and ready to go. These properties sell at higher prices, but if you don't want to deal with the complications of drilling a well on your own (or paying to dig a dry well—a worst-case scenario), then it would be smart to buy a property that already has a well and pump. We will now turn our focus to the basics of water wells, as that is the most common water source for people living off-the-grid.

What Is a Water Well and How Does It Work?

A water well is simply a hole dug or drilled into the ground that provides usable water for a property. In this chapter, we will be talking about wells drilled by a professional company. Can this be a "do-it-yourself" project? Sure, it can. But for most, including myself, a professionally drilled well is smarter. You've already got dozens of unknown variables to face while going off-the-grid, so why add another by trying to become a DIY well-driller? Thus, I will focus on how to hire a professional company to provide your property with a reliable water source.

What Makes a Good Well?

The things a well-drilling company will bring are a professional drilling rig. This is a large truck that will use metal pipe to drill down in the ground until a water source is reached. These tend to be very heavy, large vehicles. As the projected difficulty of finding underground water increases, so does the size of the truck. This is another reason having good access and reliable roads is vital for your off-the-grid project.

Indeed, you should never underestimate the importance of road accessibility for jobs that require heavy equipment. And I'm not just talking about having a road you can drive on. For example, because my roads were very steep and had loose fine dirt, the drilling rig had to be towed to the drilling site with a bulldozer. To avoid such problems, if your property is difficult to access, make sure to do a full site check with the company you plan to use. Good companies will ask in advance, but don't wait for them to do so because they might forget. If the drilling pros believe their truck will have difficulty on your roads, ask if using a bulldozer to tow the drilling rig is permitted. Drilling rigs are very expensive, and some companies will not allow them to be towed to a drilling site because of possible damage. So, it's always better to know in advance!

Also, if you can't provide a decent access road for the drilling rig, even a small one, you'll need an alternative plan to get your water. Trust me there are a ton of beautiful properties that do not have the ability, due to poor, or no road access. Some properties are ATV access only, and even then, you can only access the last part of property by foot. I have been to properties like this. They are pretty cool. But you will definitely be roughing it, and it will probably only be a part-time property. There is nothing wrong with that. I know people who have and love these types of part-year properties. But you should know what you're getting yourself into before you spend money on land.

A Common Drilled Water Well Consists of . . .

- A drilled hole.
- A casing to line the hole so it does not collapse. This casing is usually some sort of pipe—maybe four inches in diameter—that reaches down to the bottom of the well.
- An electric-powered pump to pump water to the surface.
- A well cap (which stops contaminants from entering the well).

You can expect to pay from around $50-$75 per foot of drilled well depth for all these components. This is a general guideline. It will obviously change depending on numerous factors. But I have found this to be a fairly consistent cost estimate for a professionally drilled well.

The well hole is simply a hole drilled into the ground by a drill bit attached to sections of pipe. However, these are not the same kind of wells your great-grandparents may have used back on the farm. Have you ever seen an old-fashioned well with a bucket on a rope attached to a winch? An outdated well like this might be 20 or 30 feet deep, and it would reach water caught in deep layers of mud. That's not sanitary or pleasant to drink, but it was all they had in the mid-20th Century.

In contrast, a machine-dug modern well is very deep; sometimes reaching hundreds of feet below the surface (my well is 510 feet deep). I know of some wells that are close to 1,000 feet deep. These deep wells let you reach water that has passed through the layers of dirt on the Earth's surface. Water that has filtered down to the hard bedrock beneath. This water is very clean and pure and is exquisite to drink. In fact, once you taste fresh well water you will hardly be able to believe you drank city water most of your life! So if you've ever drunk nasty well water and are turned off at the idea, don't worry. That well was either not drilled right, or not drilled deeply enough.

Note that the depth needed to find fresh water in bedrock depends on the geology of your area. In some areas of the country, you will need to dig 800 feet or more to reliably hit drinkable water. Other places require only a couple hundred feet. Well-drilling professionals will understand how deep they need to drill in order to hit bedrock. They do this by researching the depths of existing wells in your area. This is important to know ahead of time since you are charged per foot of drilling. Just remember that the more remote you are the less data there will be. It is possible there will be no data at all. In this case, you are rolling the dice a bit, because you have no idea at what depth you will reach clean drinkable water.

You'll also want to ask well drilling companies about their success rate. If you live hundreds of feet above a plentiful underground aquifer, it will be easy to drill for water. However, some areas have water running in cracks in bedrock, which must be blindly targeted from above ground to hit water. Success is not guaranteed. In such cases, if water is not discovered the first time, you may have to pay for more drilling in the future. So, ask companies about their success rate, never assume.

If you are on a tight budget or have no data to help you figure out about how deep your well needs to be, I suggest hiring a water well surveyor company. They will come to your property and conduct testing using sound waves (seismic equipment) to locate an aquifer (water-bearing rock readily transmits water to wells and springs) on your property. If you do this prior to drilling, your chances are better of getting the job done right the first time.

Another method, which I used, is a technique called witching or dowsing. Dowsing works by using dowsing rods, which is a traditional forked stick taken from a willow, peach, or witchhazel tree. Some dowsers may use keys, wire coat hangers, pliers, wire rods and pendulums. Dowsers take this stick and walk their property with one dowsing rod in each hand. When the rods come together and cross, that is the supposed location of a water source. This might sound like superstition, but dowsing has been used to find underground water sources for hundreds of years. While there is no documented scientific evidence that dowsing works, I can say that it's worked for me and numerous people I know.

Indeed, with a modern well, drilling goes as far down as necessary to reach the water supply. This supply is measured in gallons of water per minute—which is the amount of water measured when pumped from a given well. There is no absolute standard on what is considered an "adequate" amount of water. It just depends on your needs and expectations, such as how many people will be living in your house.

A workable well should produce a minimum of one gallon of water per minute. Now, I know you are thinking—that is not very much water! How would you even be able to take a shower with that low of an amount of water? We will discuss this in a moment. But first, I'd like to share my tips for picking the right people to drill your well.

Choosing a Well-Drilling Company

Water access is the key to success for your off-the-grid lifestyle. This makes choosing a good well-drilling company very important. In fact, I spent months researching local companies, and getting quotes for drilling my well. This is not something you want to mess up. That's why I'd like to share my hard-won advice about the best way to choose good well-drilling professionals.

I moved to a new state to go off-the-grid. So, unfortunately, not being from the area made it hard to find a good well drilling team. I decided to use the tried-and-true method of getting three different quotes from local drilling companies. I picked one large company out of a neighboring big city, and two small, privately-owned companies closer to my property.

Just as I do when hiring general contractors (a topic we will cover in depth in another chapter), I proceeded with great caution. I did not hear anything negative about the two small companies, which was a good sign. But I had to take that with a grain of salt, since contracting companies are notoriously unreliable—even those with good online reputations.

The two smaller companies ended up giving a lower quote than the bigger company. It wasn't much lower. Yet, even though the larger company had a higher estimate, I decided to hire them, because:

- They have been in business for almost 25 years.
- They had the most experience drilling wells in my area and in remote areas.
- They had—by far—the best equipment.
- I knew it was probable that I would need a relatively deep well, and they had a drilling rig large enough to dig a very deep well quickly and efficiently.
- They had a broader geographic reach, longer history, and bigger and more established client base. So, I knew the odds of them being in business over the long haul were far higher than the smaller privately owned companies. This was important should something go wrong with my well in the future.
- They demonstrated the most knowledge and understanding of my unique project.
- They had no problem with the difficult roads and remote location of my property.
- They were very easy to deal with and explained the entire process to me in a way that was helpful and proved they knew what they were talking about.

Fogle Pump (www.foglepump.com) is the name of the larger company I ended up going with. They are exclusive to the NE Washington and NW Idaho areas, and I'm not sure how far they travel for drilling services. However, I thought I would mention them for anyone who might be looking to drill a well in these areas. I had a positive experience with them. To this day, they have been incredibly responsive to any questions I have had. They also handled all the permitting and water testing requirements for my county, so it was a very painless process.

In the end I was glad I went with Fogle Pump, because my well ended up being 510 feet, which is pretty darn deep. They knocked it out in two days, which is also really good, because they had a powerful drilling rig that could do the job. If I had hired the smaller companies, their smaller rigs would have taken much longer to reach that depth.

As you all know, I'm all for supporting smaller, local companies. But in this case it was better to go with the bigger business that had more experience dealing with my type of property. If my land was not at the top of a mountain and hadn't required the depth of drilling that it had, I would have had no problem going with a smaller mom-and-pop company. As always, the right choice for you should depend on your situation.

What Every Off-Gridder Should Know
Gallons Per Minute and Static Water Level

No matter how professional your well-drilling team is, it's important to know that not all wells deliver the same experience at the faucet. Some wells have a larger capacity and are more powerful. Some refill faster than others, creating more reliable and powerful flow at your faucet. Some wells are slower to refill and have a smaller capacity. This leads to unreliable and weak water flow at your tap. If you've ever turned on your kitchen sink when the water pressure is low, you know why this matters. Because of this, it's important to understand the terms used to describe how effective and powerful a well is. This way, you can make an educated decision on whether you need supplementary systems to boost your well-water delivery at the faucet.

STATIC WATER LEVEL: Once you drill your well, water will typically rise upward from the absolute bottom of the well to some distance below the surface and stay there. This is called your "static water level", and it is measured in the distance from the ground down to the water in your well. For example, if the water in your well rises until it is 250 feet below ground level, your static water level is 250 feet. This is the "resting" level of water when you are not pumping and haven't pumped recently. Your official static water level is usually measured after twenty-four hours of zero pumping activity. Your drilling company will provide this number to you in their final report.

For example, my well is 510 feet down to the bottom, and my static level measured at 235 feet. So, after twenty-four hours of non-usage, 275 feet of my well shaft is filled with water, which is pretty good. Remember, your static water level is important because this reflects how much water the well shaft can store for you. For example, if your well is 500 feet deep and your static water level is 250 feet, that means your well can store a total of 250 feet of water for your use. But that's just half of the equation. The other measurement you need to know is your gallons per minute.

In terms of production, my well is on the low (dry) end and produces only three gallons per minute. While this is not especially high, my static level is good. This means that, overall, I have a good well. The odds of me using 275 feet of resting water in the well shaft in a short time period, on top of my 3 gallons per minute, is highly unlikely. If I was going to homestead, have a herd of big thirsty animals and was growing crops to eat or to sell, I might have had to change my plan.

Could I have had a more productive well drilled? Sure. I could have continued to drill until I got a higher gallon per minute measurement. But that's not what I needed. Remember, if you are going to live a simpler lifestyle you won't be watering lush lawns or extravagant landscaping. You might already live in a forest, and I do. Plus, if you plan to be completely off-the-grid, remember that a well pump relies on electricity. This means you'll be draining your off-grid power system stores if you have a big powerful pump. Very deep wells typically require the most powerful pumps to push the water to the surface. So there is a practical trade-off between depth and cost when it comes to your ongoing power needs.

Another thing you should know about wells is that depth doesn't guarantee a good well. Sometimes deeper drilling does not yield great results, and it can be costly to start over and drill again at another site. Fortunately, there is an alternate solution if you can't get adequate amounts of water from your well because of a low gallons-per-minute rate. The alternative is a water storage system.

A WATER STORAGE SYSTEM: A water storage system is exactly what it sounds like. It's a place where you store water pumped up from your primary water supply for later use. Note that this is not a water pressure or rainwater collection system. This is simply a water storage system. We will discuss water harvesting in depth later.

A water storage system consists of a plastic or metal tank with anywhere from 55 gallons to 5,000 gallons of available storage. The system uses a pump to move water from the well shaft into the storage tank for later use. So if you have a low gallon per minute rate this is a simple yet effective solution.

Water storage systems are energy efficient since your pump does not have to run continuously. In fact, your storage system does kick on every time you use water. This allows your pump to run enough to fill the tank, and then shut off. This means less power usage and less wear and tear on your pump. It takes more energy to start a water pump initially, so the more often it kicks on the more energy you will use. With a water storage system, your pump only has to kick on when the storage system needs to be refilled.

Water supply systems range from the very simple to the very complicated. If you want a hands-off approach, a small float within the storage tank can automatically trigger your pump, thereby refilling the storage tank to a specified level without any extra effort from you. In contrast, the simplest and most cost-effective method is to use gravity to carry water from the water storage tank to your house. You will, of course, need sloping land to accomplish this.

Finally, depending on how much you need to boost the water pressure available from the well, you may need additional pumps or a water pressure tank. This type of pump and store system can also be used for other types of water sources—river, creek, pond and lake.

How to Get Consistent Water Pressure at the Tap

Many off-grid homes will benefit from a system designed to maintain constant water pressure. That is, if you like to have water come out of the taps instantly when you turn them on.

A WATER PRESSURE TANK: This is simply a small tank system ranging from 20 gallon (small) to 85 gallon (large). It gives you a consistent pressure level even when you're using a little bit of water. Meaning, you get consistent pressure whether washing your hands, brushing your teeth, or doing the dishes. If you like taking long showers or doing large loads of laundry, you should get the largest water pressure tank possible. If you are a heavy water user, you can also set up multiple water pressure tanks.

These tanks keep your water pressure more consistent and give you quicker access. Meaning, a big benefit of the pressure tank is "instant" water. Without a pressure tank, it can take several seconds, or even minutes for your pressure to kick in. So, without a pressure pump, you may find yourself waiting a bit after turning on the faucet. But with a water pressure tank, you can turn on the faucet and get instant access to a good water flow.

Water pressure tanks also decrease wear and tear on your well pump, making it a good economic decision. Without a water pressure tank, your well pump will need to kick on every time you turn on the faucet. Well pumps usually cost in the range of $2,000–$2,500, not including installation. However, the less you use them, the longer they will last, making a water pressure tank a smart long-term investment

The bottom line is that your water usage is directly tied to costs, even when living off-the-grid. If you can take shorter showers, skip watering the lawn, and if you only turn on your faucet when you have to, you will extend the life of your water access system. I like this approach as I believe getting off-grid is about a simpler, more cost effective and more streamlined approach to life.

How to Get More Water When You Need it

If you want a garden and plan to grow your own food, or even start a business selling the foods you grow, you'll probably want a second water source. For such circumstances, a rainwater collection system is a great solution. Not only will you have additional water access outside of your primary water supply system, you'll drastically reduce the wear and tear on your water pumps.

So how does a rainwater collection system work? It's simple: You just collect the rainwater from your roofed buildings via a typical rain gutter system by directing it into a plastic or metal storage tank.

Obviously, if you live in a part of the world that doesn't get very much rain, this is not a viable solution. On the other hand, some areas get so much rain that people can use rainwater collection only. I have seen off-grid houses in Hawaii for example, that exclusively rely on rain water and don't have a well system at all.

A final note: Remember if you are going to collect rainwater, you will need to have an overflow to divert extra water away from the tank and your dwellings once the former is full. The last thing you want is to create water damage on your structure!

Water Filtration and Purification Basics

If you're going to live off-the-grid, you should consider getting a water filtration and purification system. There are many options, depending on the quality of your water and your personal standards.

And yes, there is a difference between water filtration and water purification. Essentially, purification keeps your water safe, while filtration keeps unwanted materials (think dirt and sediment) out of your water. Filtration alone does not guarantee your water will be safe to drink. Likewise, purification alone will not remove excess debris from your water supply. Here are some more details about the difference between water filtration and water purification. . . .

FILTRATION: A water filtration system can filter out either sediment or carbon. Most filtration systems today can perform both functions. Most also block protozoa (i.e. Cryptosporidium, Giardia) and bacteria (i.e. Salmonella, E. coli), but they might miss small viruses or pharmaceutical chemicals that have contaminated water supplies. Sadly, chemicals from pharmaceutical drugs are commonly found in today's city drinking water. This is why it's important to filter your water.

PURIFICATION: Water purification is a process that removes specific unwanted materials from your water, such as organic pollutants and chemicals. Basically, purification is an extra step that makes your water safer to drink. This is why I like the Berkey (which we will discuss more later) for drinking water, which is rated as a purifier.

Now, some people try to go off-the-grid without a water "cleaning" system. If you use a professional well drilling company, they will test your water as part of their service. So you will know beforehand whether it is safe to drink, as most counties will require this as part of the permitting process. I purify all my drinking water, but I do not filter or purify any of the well water used for non-drinking purposes. I do this because my water is incredibly clear with hardly any visible sediment, if any at all. I also leave my property for the winter, and a purification system would make my winterization process a lot more difficult. Finally, I grew up on well water and we did not have a filtration or purification system, so I'm used to using a well this way.

The downside to this approach is that you leave yourself open to possibly getting contaminates into your house water—a risk you will have to evaluate on your own.

I do recommend filtering and purify any well water which you or even your animals will drink or use in foods. It's especially important to filter and purify water exposed to outside elements, such as rainwater, streams, lakes, or ponds. I know several people who have contracted Giardia and become very ill by not filtering and purifying their water. Below are some more details about systems that I have either researched or used.

Gary's Favorite Water Preparation Systems

The simplest and cheapest system is a high-quality shower water filter, combined with a separate portable drinking water purification system. I like purifiers from *Berkey Filters* (www.

berkeyfilters.com), which are relatively inexpensive and effective. I have had good luck with them. But, as with all products, you need to test and find what works best for you. As most of you know, I'm very careful with the products I recommend. In fact, I removed a product originally included in my first edition of this book because the company had gone downhill since I first started using it. Products that work for me may also not work for you . . . that is just the way it goes.

In addition to filtering and purifying your drinking water, you should consider using a shower water filter. Why, bother with a shower filter? Your skin is the largest organ of your body, and in contradiction to popular belief, it *can* absorb harmful chemicals and microorganisms. These pollutants can then pass into your bloodstream. In fact, the damaging chemicals you can incur via your skin and lungs (from the water and steam in the shower) can do more damage than those in your unfiltered drinking water.

I have used the *Aquasana* and *Sprite HHC* (I have used the Sprite shower filter in my RV for several years now) shower filter in combination with the Berkey drinking water purification system as a cheap and easy solution for my travel trailer. This combination has worked well for me and can work as an off-the-grid water filtration/purification system for your home. This system is very economical. It runs in the $250 to $350 (that's if you're using the smaller Berkey system).

The downside to this combination is the water coming through the Aquasana and Sprite shower filter is not purified. So it is possible for pathogens to pass through it and to still be absorbed through your skin. These are mainly used to filter and soften the water and should be supplemented with more expensive systems for purifying the water.

Whole-House Water Filtering/ Purification Setup

A whole-house filtration and/or purification water system is a central system that treats water before it reaches any of your faucets or appliances. It is located between your outside water source (such as your well) and the inside water outlets.

Whole-house systems cost quite a bit more. However, they filter and/or purify all of the water entering the house, so some people prefer them. These systems can range in cost from several hundred dollars to thousands of dollars.

A basic whole-house water filter system consists of the following three filtering systems or stages:

- Stage one removes sediment.
- Stage two removes chlorine and heavy metals.
- Stage three is usually a heavy-duty carbon filter for removing hormones, drug residues, chemicals, pesticides, and herbicides.

Note that the above is only an example of a *filtration* system. You will need an additional, ultraviolet purification system to purify your water once it is filtered.

Ultraviolet water purification lamps produce UV-C or "germicidal UV". This radiation is much more intense than that of sunlight. Since UV light is the only thing capable of killing microorganisms (bacteria, viruses, molds, algae, yeast, and oocytes) most ultraviolet purification systems are combined with some type of filtration systems.

UV light generally has no impact on heavy metals or other chemical contaminants. Nevertheless, it is arguably the most cost-effective and efficient technology currently available to off-gridders. It will eliminate a wide variety of biological contaminants from your water supply.

UV water treatment offers many advantages without introducing additional chemicals to your water. These systems produce no byproducts and will not alter the pH (effects) or other properties of your water. These systems help you create safe drinking water and are not harmful to your plumbing and septic systems.

Certainly, there are other systems that can be used for filtration and purification. However, I have found the above-described system to be the simplest and most economical. I spent weeks researching every solution possible. The more time I spent on it, the more confused I became. Finally, after a ton of research, and after talking with people who had been living off-the-grid for a while, I decided on the systems we just discussed.

The Importance of Understanding Water Rights

One reason to live off-the-grid is to get as far away as possible from "The Gridmasters". I'm talking about people in the government, the corporate world, or sometimes in your private life, who seem to get off on either selling you crap you don't need or harassing you with stupid laws and regulations. Unfortunately, you still have to deal with these chumps at some level, so it's important to understand your rights, especially when it comes to water access.

Let's say, for example, you bought a property with a stream running down your hillside with the intention of using it as a water and energy source. In this case, it would be disappointing if your neighbor further upstream on the hill, whose property contained the source of the stream, decided to divert it in a completely different direction, leaving your land completely dry.

Could they legally do that? Who has the right to use or alter surface (above-ground) bodies of water? Can someone upstream significantly change the nature of a flowing water source? The answer to these questions will vary from state to state, so you need to understand your water rights before you go off-the-grid.

A water right is a legal entitlement designed to protect the use and enjoyment of bodies of water. Water rights can also govern who gets to divert water sources. Now, I could write an entire book about water rights alone. This section will give you a basic understanding of how water rights weighed into my decision to use a well as my water source—and how they might affect your decisions about water.

I grew up in the Owens Valley in California, much of which is hot and arid, meaning water access and droughts are ongoing problems. The land of my youth has a rich history of fighting Los Angeles over water rights and use (a conflict known as the California Water Wars).

The Owens Valley was once a beautiful, lush ranching and farming area. Now, it's a dry, parched desert. The drama that led to this massive change has heightened my sensitivity to water rights in general. Besides the economic and cultural loss, the unnatural lack of water in the Owens Valley led to dust storms that blew alkali dust off of the now dried-up Mono Lake. This caused me, and many others, health problems while living in the area. The dust would blow off the lake, the people would breath it in, and many ended up with allergies and asthma. The department of water and power got sued over this and they had to flood the dry lake again. In fact, one of my friends made some serious money importing water into the lake. I share this story to emphasize how important it is to be aware of your water rights.

Because I had witnessed the potential problems associated with water rights issues when dealing with above-ground water-ways (streams, rivers, and such), I decided to buy a mountain-side property with views instead of a valley property with streams. I also decided to use a well as my primary water supply.

I know people who have been in long term battles with the city, the county, and private property owners over above-ground water supplies. Not to say this is an everyday occurrence, but it does happen, so it should be a part of your off-the-grid property decision.

Water rights also apply to below-ground water sources, which is important if you install a well. Here's a quote from encyclopedia. com (with my italics) about underground water rights. . . .

> Three theories of underground water rights have evolved. The first theory, known as the absolute ownership theory, derives from English law and affords landowners the right to withdraw as much underground water as they wish, for whatever purpose, requiring their neighbors to fend for themselves. Under the second theory, known as the American rule, *landowners may withdraw as much underground water as they like* as long as it is not done for a malicious purpose or in a wasteful manner. This theory is now applied in a majority of jurisdictions in the United States.

The laws concerning above-ground water get very complicated and are more restrictive. Considering my "live free and simple" mindset, I wanted the most reliable (legal) water solution—one which would attract the least government interference. For me, this meant digging a well.

This is not to say wells are problem free. They can dry up, and can be subject to government interference and regulations. But they also have some definite benefits when you consider how the law applies to above-ground water sources.

This summary from the legal section of www.thefreedictionary. com gives you a glimpse of how complicated above-ground water rights can be. . . .

An owner or possessor of land that abuts a natural stream, river, pond, or lake is called a riparian owner or proprietor. The law gives riparian owners certain rights to water that are incident to possession of the adjacent land. Depending on the jurisdiction in which a watercourse is located, riparian rights generally fall into one of three categories.

First, riparian owners may be entitled to the "natural flow" of a watercourse. Under the natural flow doctrine, riparian owners have a right to enjoy the natural condition of a watercourse, undiminished in quantity or quality by other riparian owners. Every riparian owner enjoys this right to the same extent and degree, and each such owner maintains a qualified right to use the water for domestic purposes, such as drinking and bathing. However, this qualified right does not entitle riparian owners to transport water away from the land abutting the watercourse. Nor does it permit riparian owners to use the water for most irrigation projects or commercial enterprises. Sprinkling gardens and watering animals are normally considered permissible uses under the natural flow doctrine of riparian rights.

Second, riparian owners may be entitled to the "reasonable use" of a watercourse. States that recognize the reasonable use doctrine found the natural flow doctrine too restrictive. During the industrial revolution of the nineteenth century, some U.S. courts applied the natural flow doctrine to prohibit riparian owners from detaining or diverting a watercourse for commercial development, such as manufacturing and milling, because such development impermissibly altered the water's original condition.

In replacing the natural flow doctrine, a majority of jurisdictions in the United States now permit riparian owners to make any reasonable use of water that does not unduly interfere with the competing rights and interests of other riparian owners. Unlike the natural flow doctrine, which seeks to preserve water in its original condition, the reasonable use doctrine facilitates domestic and commercial endeavors that are carried out in a productive and reasonable manner.

When two riparian owners assert competing claims over the exercise of certain water rights, courts applying the reasonable use doctrine generally attempt to measure the economic value of the water rights to each owner. Courts also try to evaluate the prospective value to society that would result from a riparian owner's proposed use, as well as its probable costs. No single factor is decisive in a court's analysis.

Third, riparian owners may be entitled to the "prior appropriation" of a watercourse. Where the reasonable use doctrine requires courts to balance the competing interests of riparian owners, the doctrine of prior appropriation initially grants a superior legal right to the first riparian owner who makes a beneficial use of a watercourse. The prior appropriation doctrine is applied in most arid western states, including Arizona, Colorado, Idaho, Montana, Nevada, New Mexico, Utah, and Wyoming and requires the riparian owner to demonstrate that she is using the water in an economically efficient manner. Consequently, the rights of a riparian owner under the prior appropriation doctrine are always subject to the rights of other riparian owners who can demonstrate a more economically efficient use.

Under any of the three doctrines, the interests of riparian owners are limited by the constitutional authority of the state and federal governments. The Commerce Clause of the U.S. Constitution gives Congress the power to regulate Navigable Waters, a power that Congress has exercised in a variety of ways, including the construction of dams. In instances where Congress does not exercise its power under the Commerce Clause, states retain authority under their own constitutions to regulate waterways for the public good.

The ongoing drought issues in this country suggest to me that water will become an increasingly valuable resource. In fact, some of the Gridmasters are already busy buying up large supplies of fresh water and bottling it to sell for a profit. Almost everyone has seen their water bill rise dramatically over the last few years, and government-imposed restrictions on water usage are growing all the time. Water is not an unlimited resource. I would rather have the maximum control over this valuable resource by having access to well water on my property.

The downside is a well will cost you more than an above-ground water source because you will have to drill for it. However, anything in life that gives you more freedom will always come at a cost . . . in this case it's a cost I am willing to pay.

Learn more about proper well construction and safe drinking water:

https://www.epa.gov/privatewells

Off-The-Grid Septic and Sewage Disposal

YOUR POO AND PEE HAVE TO GO SOMEWHERE

One of the most confusing topics concerning off-the-grid living is dealing with human waste and its proper disposal. Remember, being off-the-grid means no access to city sewage and waste disposal system. You have to find a solution that fits within your city/county zoning and code regulations. This chapter covers the two most common and efficient systems for dealing with septic waste. I'll also give you the option I DO NOT recommend, and why.

First, don't do what your great-grandparents did. With all the environmental impact laws today, I don't recommend digging a hole and putting up an outhouse on your property without researching the applicable laws in your area. If you really want an outhouse, a simple trip to your county inspection/zoning office should get you going in the right direction and they will let you know if that option is feasible or not in your area.

Hey, nothing wrong with an outhouse. After all, people on homesteads have been using them for hundreds of years. However, things are quickly changing when it comes to waste disposal and the associated laws. So an outhouse may not be an option for many off-gridders.

To make things more confusing, current building codes regarding outhouses can change depending on the type of house you are building. Let's say you are just going to build a seasonal cabin. Many of the codes and zoning requirements are different for a vacation home than they would be for permanent residential dwelling.

Oh boy, did I just stir up the hornets' nest! Here is the key (and it's so important you'll hear me repeat it throughout this book!). . . .

Always, always check your city/county codes before you build anything, even a small tool shed. It will save you a ton of time and hassle. Not only that, building to code has many other benefits. You will likely need to pass a code inspection to get your owner occupancy certificate from the county. You'll also need to pass one if you want to open a home equity line of credit later. If you want these options available, you need to have everything, and I emphasize, *everything* done to the proper building codes for your area.

Some readers have complained about me telling them to check with your county building inspector's office instead of providing a specific list of things to be careful with. There is no possible way I could cover every building situation, for living off-grid. This book would be 100 times the length and ridiculously boring if I tried to cover everything. Even then, every area is different, and building codes are constantly being updated. So you need to practice some self-reliance here and do this old-fashioned thing called research.

Yes, I'm encouraging you to figure this one thing out on your own. The off-grid lifestyle demands self-reliance and punishes those who don't practice it. If you need me, or anyone, to tell you exactly what to do and hold your hand in everything, you're not ready to go off-the-grid yet. Then the flip side, some say it is unnecessary—just do what you want and tell the regulatory agencies to go screw themselves. Hey, I don't like unnecessary government interference in my life either. But if you ignore building codes, you will make your own life harder and have a hell of a time selling your off-the-grid property, should you decide to move. So, pick your battles wisely. There's a time and a place for civil disobedience.

Cutting corners in the beginning will cost you big time down the road. Not to mention the fact that, depending on where your neighbors are in relation to your dwelling, they might not appreciate you cutting corners on sewage disposal. I mean, how would you like your neighbor up the hill from you to install an unapproved septic system and have their waste wash down onto your property and into your drinking water? I know I wouldn't be too happy about that! Always use common sense in these matters and think of the impact your decisions will have on the environment and your neighbors. Your off-the-grid neighbor could save your life someday, or be there to offer a helping hand, so it's better not to create enemies with your poo!

Now, let's talk about the three most common solutions for your sewage and waste material. These will fulfill most city/county code requirements. (Note: Building codes literally vary by state and even by county. For example, some require a certain distance between your well site for drinking water, and septic. Always check before you build!)

Stinky Solutions

Option 1: The Standard Septic Tank

A standard holding tank septic system is good for off-grid living when city sewers are not an option. The system consists of four components:

- A pipe that carries waste from your home.
- A septic tank where solid waste is stored.
- A drain field that spreads the waste water out and away from your home.
- A microbe-containing soil for final filtering and cleaning of liquid waste.

The standard septic tank system is the most common type of system for people not hooked up to public utilities. In fact, this is the type of system my family and I used during my entire child-hood. For this type of system to be accepted and approved by your city/county, a couple of things typically need to be in place.

1. An approved engineer must design and draw the system. This proposal must be submitted to the city/county for approval.
2. Test holes must be dug at the proposed septic site, and the results of these tests must be approved by the city/county. The purpose of the holes is to make sure the below-ground geology is appro-priate for drainage; usually these holes must go six feet or deeper without hitting solid rock, so the liquid waste has an adequate drainage area.

3. All the proposed building materials for the system must be approved by the city/county prior to final installation.

So, where should you put your septic drain area (also known as the septic field)? Note that some types of ground topography make it unlikely that your septic system will be approved. For example, if you are high on a steep slope, or near a main river, local building codes may make it impossible to get a permit. Codes may also be somewhat arbitrary. For example, they might not be clear on how many yards must be between your septic field and your closest neighbor.

Also, many building codes don't allow any structures to be built on *top* of septic fields. In other words, you shouldn't put your septic field in the exact spot where you plan an outbuilding, solar array, or pergola-covered patio. This is something you'll want to check with your city or county about *before* you build.

So the best place for your septic system is usually downhill from your home. This way gravity moves waste from toilet to tank, and eventually to the drain field. This is normally called a gravity flow system. If you cannot use gravity and/or cannot find a deep enough area for the drain field, you will have to use a pressure-based septic system.

Option 2:
The Pressure Distribution Septic System

A pressure distribution septic system is made up of five major components:

1. A dosing tank that collects liquid discharge.
2. A pump that moves the liquid out of the dosing tank and into the drain field.
3. Controls for floats, and a timer to turn the pump on and off.
4. Manifolds to distribute the septic liquid discharge to lateral lines.
5. Lateral lines with holes that evenly distribute the liquid into drain field.

This type of system will have to go through the same city/county-approval process as previously outlined for the standard septic tank system.

Compared to a standard gravity-fed septic system, a pressure distribution system is far more complex, but in the end does the same thing. The pressure distribution system costs much more, but it gets the job done when your dirt is too shallow for a gravity-fed system to work.

Today (2020), on average, a gravity-fed system is in the $5,000 to $7,500 range, fully installed by a professional, including engineering drawings and permits. In contrast, back in 2014 time frame, I received two quotes for a pressure distribution system in the $15,000 to $17,000 range.

For cost and ease of use, you ideally want to use a standard gravity-fed system. The only reason you might want a pressurized system is if your property does not meet the drain-field depth and/or gravity-feed requirements. That's something to consider when buying your off-grid property! Here is the snag. . . .

Even if you have a great gravity-fed system site, an unscrupulous installer may try to talk you into the pressurized system, because they can make more money off you . . . a lot more money!

If I hadn't grown up in a rocky, mountainous area similar to my current off-grid Washington property, I'd have no clue that installing a standard gravity system was even an option.

The first two local septic installers I spoke to tried to sell me some song and dance about my property not being ready to support a standard gravity-fed system. But, I was familiar with how these systems worked, so I knew better. I finally found a septic installer with some integrity who agreed with me, and the standard system was installed without any problems. So, beware of anyone who tries to sell you a pressure distribution system, because they might be full of shit (no pun intended . . . ok maybe a little!).

Basically, the two previous idiot installers were trying to "small town" me. They thought I knew nothing about septic systems. Needless to say, they are now on Gary's shit list and will not be getting any business or referrals from me. On that note, I will cover how to deal with these "Joe Six-Pack" contractors later on in this book.

There are many technical variations on gravity-fed and pressure distribution systems. But, they are certainly the two most common systems for off-grid living. Both of these can be a "do-it-yourself" project, although you should, again, check with your city/county requirements first. Be aware also that creating a septic field involves a whole lot of digging around in the dirt.

In my situation, once I factored in the time and cost, it was easier to have a professional do it. This also gave me the added insurance that if anything goes wrong, they will fix it. There are certain projects that are out of my comfort zone, and when it comes to poo and pee, I would rather have a professional involved.

Option 3: What About Composting Toilets?

I saved my very favorite for the last: the option that I like to call "pooping in a bucket". If you are still reading after that comment, know that I have nothing against making your own composting toilet. But it's honestly just a bucket with a toilet seat, and some saw dust. I have used them, and they work just fine. In some cases, a composting toilet will be your only option.

But, for now, I will focus on professionally made compost toilets. A homemade option is what I consider a camping/hunting toilet. It doesn't take much skill to build one either, so don't rule that out.

There are two main types of professionally built composting toilets:

1. Central
2. Self-contained

A central composting toilet has a separate composter, which requires gravity to get waste to a separate composter. The central composting toilet is usually located in a basement or crawl space. A self-contained composting toilet is smaller, and the toilet and composter (where solids are broken down) are combined into one unit.

They both break down solid biological waste without using water.

While they can be far more environmentally friendly than most waste disposal systems, they can also be expensive and a bit of a pain in the butt. I considered using a composting toilet, but quickly found it would be a complete waste of money for my situation, because:

- They are pretty expensive—costs range from $2,000 to $3,000. I installed two standard toilets and had a modern gravity-fed septic system professionally installed for around the same price as two consumer model composting toilets.

- Some composting toilets have a lot of parts and are hard to install. Imagine spending days messing with a complicated IKEA version of a toilet.

- They are massive. I think the term "sitting on the throne" must have been coined by someone using one of these things.

- They stink. I read review after review about people who bought them, and the biggest complaint was they smell as you would expect: like poo!

- In order for them to work correctly you have to pee in a separate container, which you'll have to empty manually.

- They only solve one problem, which is the collection and break down of waste. After that, you still have a big container of waste which you'll need to dispose of per city/county code.

- In some cases, they do not meet city/county code requirements.

- They are highly temperamental. If the temperature is not kept in a consistent range, the bacteria will not compost solids.

- Some use electricity to aid the composting process. Since living off-the-grid means using as few electricity-sucking appliances as possible, a composting toilet might not be economically smart.

This is why I didn't use a composting toilet. Why should you when there are other systems which take care of human biological waste and keep dirty water out of your house? Your biological waste is just one of many things that go down the drain, water for house cleaning, showers, washing dishes, laundry, and so on.

Some people prefer composting toilets because they think the environmental impact is less. I applaud them for that. But I think you can be environmentally friendly, successfully go off-the-grid, and still have some of the creature comforts you are used to. Starting with a modern septic system.

CHAPTER 7

Don't Get Small-Towned by Joe Six-Pack
MY EXPERIENCES AND BRUTAL HONESTY

When I first wrote this chapter, I had no idea the firestorm it would cause. Most readers love this chapter, but I also received some nasty emails from the people I obviously called out. Either way, I'm not trying to stir anything up. I'm just sharing my decades of experience dealing with general contractors—the good ones and bad ones. Just like anything in life, no trade or job sector is immune from "bad apples". It appears some people in the general contracting industry have a bit of a thin skin. I would say they are more than likely the bad ones—and I have some good reasons for it. Bad apples hate when you call them out. Why else would someone waste their time, giving the book a bad review, or sending me a nasty email espousing how I'm being a dick, and don't know what I'm talking about?

I was in the federal government and law enforcement for a large part of my life. I have heard all kinds of stories of abuse of power, and individual's rights being violated by the bad apples in law enforcement agencies. You know why I don't go crazy publicly responding to other's blogs, giving 1-star book reviews, sending nasty emails, and wasting my time on social media screaming about how they are completely wrong and I'm "one of the good ones"? Because I KNOW I'm not a part of the problem. I was one of the good guys. Yes, I realize there are bad people in law enforcement.

But I just go on with my life, and don't let their actions change how I live. And I certainly don't get pissed off at people who complain about the bad apples. If someone is defensive and has a problem with being called out, it's probably because they're part of the problem. Such people are rarely self-reliant enough to do anything more than take shortcuts. They certainly aren't the type of people to follow through on my advice. So, if anything I say in this chapter, or book offends you, the off-the-grid lifestyle is probably not for you.

So, why include a chapter on dealing with general contractors? Well, I have been dealing with general contractors for twenty-five years now. My first business was owning and selling real estate—I had my Realtor's license for eight years. I have owned multiple types of properties, including flips, small apartment complexes, and raw land. I'm also building my fourth house from scratch right now. I'm no amateur in this area, so before you start pecking away on your keyboard, realize I had to learn these skills over decades by firing more contractors than I can count and by going back to fix their crappy work. Matter of fact, I have been offered several jobs in the construction industry by general contractors who have seen my work.

If I had the time and energy, I'd do all my own contracting work. But, since I don't (and I'm sure you don't either), we need to know how to hire contractors as if we were a real employer hiring an employee. I could write an entire book about my experiences dealing with general contractors and the horror stories others have shared with me. But there are plenty of TV shows you can watch on this topic, so no need, this chapter will suffice. Simply put, the good general contractors nod their head and laugh when they read this chapter. If you're one of them, I'll be the first to say that I'm damn glad you're out there. The bad ones get their underwear all bunched up. But this chapter is not for contractors. It's for people who deal with general contractors while pursuing their off-the-grid project.

Urban legends about dealing with bad contractors are notoriously plentiful, and most do not have a happy ending. In fact, the hiring and management of a general contractor can be so risky and time-consuming that's why I have devoted this entire chapter to the topic. I hope this advice will spare you the all-too-common headaches and save you from the expenses and the humiliation of being ripped off.

Let's face it: There are numerous websites and even TV shows portraying the horror-story-of-the-day concerning home improvement and new house construction. Many marriages have ended, properties have been foreclosed on, and financial ruin has been caused by dishonest general contractors. If you're a good contractor or married to one, I hope you also have a good laugh, because I KNOW you deal with your fair share of bad contractors in your line of work.

That said, dealing with contractors is the most difficult part of the building process for would be off-gridders . . . period! Hiring people to help with your project is a smart move for many reasons.

Unless you're a badass contractor already, only a moron or an egomaniac tries to do all the contracting work themselves.

The people who claim to have built their off-grid house 100 percent themselves (which I question anyway) are almost always general contractors, or in the construction field. And I'll tell you first hand that building a house all on your own without any help is not realistic. Even those hardened farmers who lived primarily a life of self-reliance 150 years ago had neighbors and family members help them on building projects. You are more than likely in a remote location, where medical help could be very far away . . . this is incredibly dangerous, and I would say very stupid. This is why I laugh at these emails from people scolding me as a "hypocrite" for using contractors. If you hire experts to take care of things so you can focus your energy on other things, I call that smart entrepreneurship.

On top of my building experience, I also have many friends in the business, so I have an outside and an inside perspective to the industry. Yet even with my vast experience and with my background in law enforcement, I'm still not immune to being duped by a dishonest builder. Every industry has its share of "professional conmen", who will say and do anything to steal your hard-earned money and waste your time with nonsense and shoddy work.

Here's the tricky part: There is no perfect system to picking a contractor. It's truly buyer beware. On top of this, you can make a good contractor's experience much better by learning how to communicate and to deal effectively with them. In fact, if you have to use contractors to help you build your off-the-grid property, it will be the hardest part of the project. But if you know how to do it, you will be more mentally prepared to deal with the issues of construction as they arise. The good ones will also remember you and be much more cooperative and helpful if you need them again.

Now, even if you have the best contractor on the planet, when it comes to building a house—things are going to go wrong. That is just the way it is. The good news is, in almost all cases, these problems can be corrected. No matter how complicated a job seems, when you break any building project down, it's a basic box structure created mostly of wood, steel, and concrete. The trick is understanding how all the pieces fit together, and some contractors are much more knowledgeable than others. Add to this the common problems with human communication today, and you've got a potentially unstable scenario.

So, here is my hard-earned advice about making the most of this difficult situation.

Meet Joe Six-Pack

Remember that time you hired a roofer, plumber, electrician, carpenter, or painter, and it turned into a nightmare? He pulled up to your house and parked his two-ton diesel truck right on top of your flowerbed. Then, he tracked mud into your house, dropped a cigarette butt (still lit) onto your driveway, and stank up your spare bathroom for days. After listening to a 20-minute story about his latest DUI, he leaves you with half the job undone, and dodges your calls for two weeks before stumbling back in and half-assing the rest of his way through it . . . that is, if he even shows up again!

Okay, I'm exaggerating a little. But I just described your typical Joe Six-Pack contractor who we've all had to deal with at least once. If you're a contractor yourself, I KNOW you've cleaned up after this guy. You've covered his shifts, apologized to customers on his behalf, and been repeatedly bored out of your mind by his 30-minute diatribes about his personal problems.

Yes, we all meet Joe Six-Pack at some point in our life. The trick is to spot him coming a mile away and avoid hiring him in the first place. This is tricky, because sometimes ole Joe Six-Pack shows up in a nice clean truck with polished shoes, a silver clipboard and a slick-tongued sales pitch about why you need to buy the most expensive service he has to offer.

Meanwhile, when it comes to building your off-grid home, we are talking about one of the biggest decisions and financial investments you will make in your lifetime. So I think it is important to understand the mindset of the average Joe Six-Pack contractor, as understood from my background and experience.

I grew up with, worked with, and have employed numerous construction professionals. I also have a multi-decade background working as a professional investigator. So I have developed a good sense of the general profile of Mr. Joe Six-Pack. Such people make life hard for you, me, and for honest hard-working contractors alike. Unfortunately, the construction industry is filled with many, many people who are looking to take advantage of us, John and Jane Q. Public. This is no secret; as I said previously, you've probably had these same experiences and/or read about them or seen them in documentaries.

These bad contractors aren't just bad at their job, they half-ass everything in their life. Joe Six-Pack is the guy who occasionally attended high school, usually to hangout in the back of class and catch up on some sleep. He loved to go to all the parties, but never had any beer . . . that is, until he found yours! He always showed up at festive occasions, but always seemed to forget his wallet when the bill came. He may have actually graduated from high school . . . barely. But, he had no ambitions beyond that. He only works because he needs to (sometimes) pay bills. Combine this with his lack of work ethic and his knack for getting fired from every low-end job and you have another Joe Six-Pack in the making.

After getting kicked out of the house and running out of friends' couches to sleep on, Joe only had one recourse. . . become a general laborer in the construction industry. Again, if you know an honest hard-working person who is in construction, ask them if they know who I'm talking about. They'll tell you stories, believe me. Let's face it, you really don't need a résumé to become a laborer in construction, and you can get fired repeatedly without it hurting your chances of future employment in the industry. If you have two arms and two legs, you can and will get hired as a "warm body" laborer. True, this can be honorable work, since you're building someone's house. But remember, Joe Six-Pack is just there for the money to buy a $100,000 fishing boat and kegerator he can't really afford . . . probably ever. I know, I did a lot of menial labor as a teenager (pretty much zero knowledge in much of anything) and young adult, so not only have I done the work, I worked right next to future or current Joe Six-Pack. As a matter of fact, I have had laborers show up on projects with literally zero skills, who had been working in the industry for years. If you work in the building industry, just picture those guys who spend half the day looking for their hammer. That's who we're talking about.

Another characteristic of Joe Six-Pack is his past, current, or ongoing drug and/or alcohol problems. I have no idea why, but the general labor industry seems to be a magnet for people with substance abuse and alcohol issues. On several of my projects, I have found empty booze bottles and drug paraphernalia on the job site. To say I was a very unhappy camper with these incidents would be an understatement.

Of course, I empathize for those with substance addictions. But at some age you have to grow up and become self-reliant; or stay stuck in Peter Pan land forever. Growing up, I quickly learned that showing up on the job site hung over, or even doing drugs or drinking at work was very much the wrong path in life. If someone like me, who has done more than his fair share of stupid crap, learned that lesson early on, there's no reason someone else can't learn it too.

Joe Six-Pack never learned this lesson because he loves to blame others for his problems. Even if he installed that window incorrectly, or half-assed the dry wall project, somehow it's your fault. He is going to charge you for the crap work and leave you to fix it yourself, or live with it as is.

"Professional" Profile of Joe Six-Pack

- He has no work ethic.
- He doesn't respect your property.
- He shows up late . . . sometimes never.
- He will tell you anything to get the job.
- He is dishonest . . . and I mean very dishonest.
- He has substance abuse problems.
- He has zero organizational skills.
- He is incapable of following any type of schedule.
- He is always available and never has anyone waiting in line for his crappy services.
- He is the master of cutting corners and doing subpar work.
- He lacks proper tools to do the job and uses yours without your permission.
- He will purposefully do things wrong in order to create more work and charge you for it.

This list is more than just a rant. It's a checklist for hiring (and firing) contractors. People with professional problems typically have personal problems, and vice versa. This might sound a little bitter of me, but I'm actually pretty easygoing in general. Still, anyone who has had to deal with contractors on a regular basis is laughing their ass off as they read this list. They know what I say is true. And actually, I'm being nice to Joe Six-Pack in keeping this list short. As I said earlier, I could write an entire book with numerous "colorful but true" stories about dealing with awful contractors. It would be therapeutic for me, but you probably wouldn't get much out of it except some painful and cringe-worthy laughs. So let's move on to some concrete tips, shall we?

Now that I have completely destroyed your faith in all humanity (or at least those who lose their hammers), I will share some ways to deal with Joe Six-Pack, should you perchance employ such a social skid mark. Moreover, later on I will also give you some tips on finding the right contractor for your project. So, this is not just another Gary rant. Let's start with some quick glossary terms for those of you who haven't hired a construction team before. . . .

On a building site, the general contractor (GC) is the man (or woman) in charge. You hire him and pay him, and he (in theory) hires and pays the people under him and completes the job. The people under him might be employees who regularly work for him. These are independent contractors who bring their own gear and supplies to complete a specific part of the job. Some are specialist contractors (sub-contractors) whom your GC hires to complete some skilled work on the site. Sub-contractors on a house might include an electrician or roofer, who may often bring their own teams with them.

In theory, the general contractor's insurance and oversight should extend to his employees and subs. That is, if the GC has all the paperwork in order and does things by the book! You can usually operate as a GC on your own building project, or you can hire a GC and let him take care of the details. Note that the regulations and educational requirements for GCs vary wildly by state and sometimes even by county. I encourage you to check out what the local regulations are for your building site so you are ahead of the curve before hiring anyone posing as a GC.

A final note to drive the point home: Some states/counties have no requirements for someone becoming a GC, such as minimal years of supervised experienced or passing a written test. All that is required in some areas is paying a licensing fee, and boom; they now hold a General Contractors license. I kid you not. I'm not a big fan of unnecessary licensing and bureaucracies, but holy you-know-what, I think it is pretty important to have some experience and go through some sort of process before I pay you to build something that could fall down and kill me!

Taming Joe Six-Pack

Hopefully, this book will help you avoid hiring a bad contractor. But, let's say you end up with the notorious Joe Six-Pack as your general or sub-contractor. There are ways to still get the work done properly and on budget. Warning: Supervising a marginally competent contractor will be a real time-suck. This should be avoided if possible. Finding the right contractor is always the best way to go, even if it costs more and takes a little more time. Also, if you suspect early on that you've got a Joe Six-Pack type on your hands, and you can still fire them, do it. Don't hang on hoping they'll get better, because they never do.

Nevertheless, sometimes you get stuck with Joe Six-Pack, and you have to make lemonade from lemons. For example, in the past I have had time-sensitive building projects that needed to get done, and I've had to go with the only contractor available. Under this scenario, you almost always end up with some version of Joe Six-Pack. My advice is to fire him as soon as you possibly can to avoid future pain—which will definitely come in some form or other.

Here are my tips to managing the Joe Six-Pack of the construction world. This list is not all-inclusive, and not a guarantee of success. However, I have found these tips useful when dealing with marginally competent builders. Remember, our buddy Joe Six-Pack doesn't follow the rules and is highly unpredictable. So even the most stringent fail-safes may not work. But here are a few general guidelines:

- Get everything in writing.
- Make sure all bids for work contain "a no higher than" cost cap.
- Get a lien release agreement (a.k.a. lien waiver) for him and all sub-contractors. (This prevents a GC or sub-contractor from applying a lien against your property if he feels you still owe him money).
- Purchase all materials yourself. (This avoids inflated costs for otherwise inexpensive materials). It also lets you control the materials, because Joe Six-Pack loves to over purchase materials on your dime, and then use them on other projects or take them home.
- Set a pre-determined schedule for completed work.
- Pay for work only when completed (Joe Six-Pack hates this one)—again, have the payment schedule in writing before you begin.
- Babysit Joe Six-Pack by never letting him out of your sight while on the job. (Set up a lawn chair and read a book next to him if you have to!)

- Avoid engaging him in conversation outside the scope of the project. (This is his way of padding his hours and charging you for chitchat). He's not your buddy. He's an employee. If he sees you as an employer, he'll be less likely to push your boundaries.

These tips are useful when working with good contractors too. I have hired multiple contractors who started out great, but quickly became bad as the project progressed. This is part of the bad contractor's scheme: to get you to let your guard down (Stockholm syndrome comes to mind), and then take advantage of your kindness. Good contractors, on the other hand, are good throughout the entire project, as they value you as a future reference. Joe Six-Pack is purely "widget in, widget out" when it comes to getting the job done. He could care less about referrals.

Here is one last nugget of information: Joe Six-Pack loves out-of-towners, as they will not know anything about his past and (total lack of) work ethic. Moreover, I have found that in small towns, people really don't like to talk negatively about anyone, even a local company. The reasons for this are obvious. It's a small community. Everyone knows each other. So they do not want to talk badly about anyone as it can come back on them. Bad contractors know this and definitely take advantage of it.

As a matter of fact, I had to deal with this lack of small-town candor with my off-grid project, as I had to terminate my first contractor. I thought I had done the best I could to locate a good contractor by getting a referral list from the county building inspector's office. I looked into his background, not real deep, but didn't find anything negative. I also couldn't find anyone with anything negative to say about him (most people had never heard of him and that should have been the first red flag). Of course, the red flags started to appear about halfway through my project. By then people started to give their honest opinion. But by that time, I had found out the truth on my own.

Of course, my warnings are not exclusive to contractors. There are bad apples in every profession. But building a house is one of the biggest life decisions you will ever make. So it tends to have a much larger impact if things do go badly. Now that you've been thoroughly warned about Joe Six-Pack, let's talk about how to find someone you can trust to do a great job.

How to Find a Good Contractor

Now that I have completely scared you away from ever using a contractor or building a house off-the-grid, there is some good news!

There are plenty of good contractors out there! In fact, if you're one of them (or married to one), you've probably been amused at my little rant about the bad apples. Believe me, I know these people drive you crazy too. But the good contractors are out there. It just takes a little more time and energy to find them. A good contractor will make your building experience go as smoothly as possible. As I said above, things often go wrong during construction projects. That is just the way it goes. Unhelpful weather, supplier issues, unforeseen problems with the building site, and other surprises can and do happen. But a good contractor will work with you, fix their mistakes, and make it right. A bad one will blame everything on you and charge you an exorbitant price to fix it so they can have more weekend beer money.

The best and most reliable way to find a good contractor is by referral. Of course, there are numerous websites like www.angieslist. com, which can be helpful. But those don't really work in more rural areas because people just don't use them as much. Some "referral" sites aren't even what they claim to be. They're just marketing platforms where the contractor pays to be listed and recommended on the website.

It can be even more difficult to find a competent contractor for an off-the-grid home, as this is a highly specialized project. To be honest, finding contractors for my off-the-grid project has been more difficult than I expected because most contractors are only familiar with traditional construction. This is why it's important to take your time and do lots of research and asking around.

Now, as I explained previously, most people in small towns will not say anything negative about a local contractor or company. Especially if they do not know you well. The way around this is to find the local people who have recently had houses built or renovation work done. These are the folks you want to ask for referrals. If they had a negative experience, they will usually not give you the name of the builder. If they had a good experience, they will gladly give you the name of the company or contractor.

If you can't find anyone in town who has had construction work done recently, try asking for referrals at the local building supply stores. Call a few of these referrals and see if any one name gets mentioned several times—this is a good sign. Of course, this is not the ideal way to get referrals compared to the previous method. Building supply stores know who is busiest, but not necessarily who is best. But if this is your only option, it's better than nothing.

One last way, that I have had success with in more than one instance—go to the local Real Estate offices and ask who they recommend. Make sure you tell them about your project, primarily that it is going to be off-the-grid. Real estate agents usually manage properties, on top of listing and selling houses. So they usually have a good list of GCs, and people in the building trades they use on a regular basis.

How to Get Estimates/Bids

Good contractors will gladly give you an estimate/bid for your project. It's part of doing business. The good ones will also have an organized and detailed estimate/bid process in place.

A big red flag for a bad contractor is giving you your estimate/bid handwritten on a piece of paper and/or charging for their time to do an estimate/bid. Another red flag is a lack of detail on materials and costs for each phase of the project. Contractors who can't (or won't) tell you these things are either too incompetent to predict how the project will go, or they're trying to hide the real project costs. So ask questions, and make sure your prospective contractor can give you the details you need. We are all human and get excited to start a new project. With our newfound excitement, we sometimes cut corners and do other things that we wouldn't usually do—such as not getting enough bids. The goal is to get at least three bids from three different contractors before making a final decision. I have taken short cuts on getting three estimates/bids on projects in the past, and it has bit me in the butt every time. This is very important: Never ever share the bid details of one contractor with another prior to them bidding the project. If you do, their bid may not be the "right" bid, but rather the bid that they think will win them the job. I have made this mistake more than once and have gotten back a bid slightly lower or almost exactly the same as the contractor's bid information I shared.

Some contractors just use a bid to get their foot in the door. Many times, what you end up paying will be much more. It works like this. You get a bid from one contractor. The next contractor underbids by a little bit, and the low bid is usually the worst contractor of the bunch. Some of them will even subcontract your project to the shittiest subcontractor after winning the job, and just skim money off the project without being involved. Others agree to do the job for one amount, and then bloat the job up with more hours once you're locked in. Some do both. Others will underbid simply because they're morons. Early on, I hired someone to build my storage/solar shed, which I could have done myself, but was trying to save some time. Half way through the project, he decided he had under bid the project and told me "it just wasn't worth his time." Problem was, he had a bit of Joe Six-Pack in him—he actually bid the job correctly, but his inability to plan and manage the project caused it to take far longer than it should have. Needless to say, I fired him immediately, and finished the shed myself. This is another good lesson in how pulling out of a bad decision quickly can save you a LOT of time, money, and anxiety.

Here are three more reasons to get multiple estimates/bids:

1. Having more bids gives you a better idea of what your project is going to cost.

2. Having more bids keeps your contractors honest by giving you something to compare your project to. If you have multiple bids, you can ask specific questions on prices and material differences. This is especially useful if costs increase during the project.

3. Getting multiple bids slows down the contractor hiring process. This way, you don't jump into your project too quickly or without all the information. You don't know what you don't know, at least not yet. So treat your bid gathering as an education opportunity.

In addition to getting a professional and detailed quote, here are some more things to look for when searching for a good contractor.

Traits of a Good Contractor

- They provide everything in writing.
- They will not take a deposit or start work until everything is agreed to in a signed contract.
- Their contract reads like a proper legal document and allows for contingencies (clauses that detail how unusual circumstances will be handled, such as if you want to exit the contract, or if the contractor needs to make a substantive change to the original plans).
- They are highly organized and professional.
- Their new business comes primarily by referral.
- They do a lot of local work because they get a lot of referrals.
- They'll provide references for past work (e.g., phone numbers for previous customers) without being asked.
- They are prompt and on time.
- They are well known (in a good way) in the local community.
- They return your phone calls promptly. They actually use their voicemail.
- They're usually not available immediately (like tomorrow). They might have several weeks or months of projects already lined up. This is a sign of a good reputation.
- They'll be licensed with the state or county licensing board (requirements vary by state and county). They'll display their official license number on their business card, work truck, or will provide these upon request.
- They carry both general liability and worker's compensation insurance (requirements may vary by state).
- They're bondable or (better yet) bonded (protects the consumer if contractor fails to complete the job).
- They're happy to show you their certificates of insurance. Their policies will also be current.

- They have a portfolio of previous work you can look at (this may be a book of photos, or even on their website).

In very rural areas, it may be impossible to find a GC that ticks all these boxes. But don't get too obsessed with perfection. The idea is to hire someone with as many of these qualities as you can and to take your time looking for them.

A final note about licensing: GC licensing requirements vary greatly from state to state. Some states have rigorous, notoriously difficult exams and require character references to acquire a GC license. Others only have licensing at the local level, while still others have no requirements for GC licensing at all. I strongly recommend you spend some time online to get a sense of what it really means when someone calls themselves a "licensed" contractor in the area you plan to build in. You never know. They may just be talking about their fishing license.

Why Finding a Contractor for an Off-The-Grid Project is Tricky

Building an off-the-grid home is, in many ways, its own animal. There really is no template. It will be a unique experience for everyone because we all want different things. It will probably be a unique experience for your builder too. Especially since the vast majority of small-home and off-grid construction is done by contractors who only have experience with traditional building. Even with smaller scale and more remote homes becoming more popular, this is still the case.

The simple fact is that you will have to be much more involved in an off-grid construction project than you would in the building of a regular home. There are some small companies throughout the country that specialize in green/off-grid construction. But their services usually come at a lofty premium. For most of us, this just isn't an option.

The bottom line is that you will have to find a general contractor who is flexible and open to trying something new. However, it's more than likely that you will not know if this is the right contractor for the project until you are well into it. After firing my first contractor, I found a jack-of-all-trades helper who was referred by someone who had done other work for me. This made me the GC for my own project. So, even though I didn't find the right person the first time around, I made a good decision by letting them go early. One lesson I have learned is to be slow to hire and quick to fire: If things don't seem to be going in the right direction, move fast and let the contractor/helper go.

From my experience, and from what I have learned through others who have gone down this road, building off-the-grid is challenging. Many mistakes will be made. It's just the way it is.

Building Permits—Why You Need Them

This section is not intended to cover all the building requirements you will have to follow for your project. They change from state to state, county to county, and city to city. Our goal in this section will be to help you understand them and find the information you need quickly. Building codes are rules that specify the minimum standards for constructed objects—such as buildings. Codes are typically developed nationally, optionally adopted by states, and enforced locally. When something is built "to code" it means the structure meets the set of codes that your local authority (e.g. municipality, city, or county) has opted to enforce. Codes might seem like a hassle. But they're intended to protect consumers. A good contractor will know and understand all local codes so that your structure will pass inspection by the local building inspector.

Now, building codes are constantly changing, so they are moving targets. As a matter of fact, I have found that today's building codes are so confusing, most inspectors don't understand or know them all (another reason to beware of Joe Six-Pack). That can be good and bad, depending on the situation. But one thing I can guarantee is that it's best to follow the codes. If you try and "work" the system and somehow get around the local code and inspection requirements, your efforts will most likely come back to haunt you.

Here's an example of what I mean. In some cases, people simply buy a piece of land, throw up a structure, and live freely, unencumbered by any building codes or environmental regulations. Although this freestyle building approach may sound tempting, I don't recommend it. It looks good on TV, but in reality it creates a lot more stress than it is worth. Who wants to be looking over their shoulder all the time, wondering if the county is going to hit you with fines, or a whole host of other penalties for not following the rules? Build to code today and tomorrow will be less stressful.

When it Comes to Codes, Following the Rules is Smart

Yes, rules can suck. But I have found the county inspector's offices in rural communities to be very easy to work with. Why does this matter? Because before you start building, you will need to submit your building plans to the county for approval. This is not free, and the price varies depending on where you are located. For me, the entire process was around $1,500 for permits. This didn't include the engineering fees for my building plans. It appears that my permit fees will be about the same for my next grid-tied building project—which is in another state.

Here are some advantages to doing things right by getting the proper permits:

- You will have less undue stress.
- Properly permitted properties are worth far more than unpermitted properties.
- Regular inspections can save you money by catching errors in your construction process. Think of a building inspector as an impartial third-party who is (in theory) an expert at catching potentially expensive and dangerous mistakes made by contractors.
- You can weed out bad contractors by double-checking their work. This can save you time and money and keep Joe Six-Pack out of your life.

Even though you are going off-the-grid, you still have to look at your property as an investment. By cutting corners and not following the proper building processes, you only hurt yourself. What happens if something unexpected occurs, and you need to sell your property quickly? If it is an unpermitted property that is not built to code, the chances of you selling it quickly are almost zero. The worst thing is that you have now greatly reduced the value of your property.

When I first started looking for land for my off-grid project, I looked at numerous properties with unpermitted do-it-yourself houses. And almost all of them were complete wrecks. The amount of time and money it would take to bring these houses up to code was nowhere close to being worth it. In fact, I wouldn't even look at properties like this after a while. To me, a majority were scams, since most of the sellers were up-charging for the equivalent of a crappy shack. All in hopes of finding a buyer who didn't know anything about sound construction principles or building codes.

The bottom line is that, before buying any rural property with a home, outbuildings, or garage, make sure the structure has the right permitting. This applies to structures related to alternative energy sources, such as a solar panel array, about which we will discuss more later. Matter of fact, since I originally published this book, I have received numerous emails from people who bought previously constructed off-grid homes, and wasted tens-of-thousands of dollars and hundreds of hours fixing problems. Due diligence is key when it comes to these types of properties.

A good real estate agent will be able to find out whether or not a structure is properly permitted. Hopefully they will know even before you look at the property, saving you time. If your Realtor can't tell you this, just go to the county assessor's office, and they will be able to either tell you or send you in the right direction.

As far as I'm concerned, if the dwellings on a piece of land are not permitted, they are nothing more than worthless structures. If you buy one, you are only negotiating for the value of the land itself. Trust me, in most cases it's easier to start yourself from scratch than to try and salvage work which was probably done by a Joe Six-Pack.

I will leave you with one last piece of wisdom: Technology is at a point where you will eventually get caught for building an unpermitted or unapproved structure. That thing called Google Earth is pretty sophisticated these days. For example, I can go to the county technology office and get full color overhead shots of my property to help me figure out my property lines. If this is possible in the sparsely populated, rural area I'm in, I'm pretty sure it is available almost anywhere. I have heard of people sneaking structures on their property only to get caught and smacked with a nice back-tax bill . . . don't be that person!

As you can see, dealing with contractors and getting your property built can be very time consuming and stressful. Unless, of course, you do it properly. The main piece of advice I want to leave you with is to take your time. I have spoken with several people who are doing or have done what I've done with my off-the-grid property, and all have taken years to complete their projects. To date, I have yet to meet or talk to a person who has completed such a project in one season/year. I would say, on average, it takes anywhere from 3-5 years to complete an off-grid project such as mine. Of course, if you have everything organized and are sitting on a heap of cash, you might be an exception to this rule. But in most instances, you'll need to be patient. Believe me, the outcome is worth it!

Now, I know at least a few readers are thinking . . .

"Geez Gary, this sounds like a lot of work. I think I'll just buy a tiny house and put it on my property."

I know this is a popular idea these days. But you'll want to read this next chapter before following the crowd on this one . . .

The Tiny House Movement

A GOOD ALTERNATIVE OR JUST ANOTHER FAD?

hen I first published this book in 2017, the tiny home movement was in full swing. There were numerous TV shows, magazines, and websites dedicated to living the tiny home lifestyle. It appears it has cooled off a bit since then, but it is still pretty popular today for those looking to simplify their life. So what exactly is a tiny home? It's a house that is constructed on a rolling chassis (like a travel trailer) or a permanent home that is 500 square feet or less in size.

The base upon which mobile tiny homes are constructed—the aforementioned moveable chassis—is a steel frame with wheels, pretty much like a utility trailer that you would tow behind your vehicle. Some people buy plans that show them how to build the tiny house on top of the rolling chassis. Others do it themselves or pay a company to build the house to their specifications.

Tiny homes are primarily built with standard wood framing/ stick construction, like a typical wooden framed-in house you might see built on a plot of land. Yet, many mobile tiny homes are built right on top of the moveable chassis. These tiny homes are usually under 8.5 feet wide and vary in length from 12 to 24 feet. They're also restricted to 13.5 feet in height so they can fit under highway underpasses when being moved.

What Everyone Should Know About Tiny Houses

The primary reasons these tiny homes are popular has to do with them being mobile like a travel trailer but cheaper than a standard home. Makes sense right? But, just like anything trendy, there is usually hype and little substance behind the claims. In my view, mobile tiny homes are usually not the best option for off-gridders and simplified living enthusiasts because:

- Tiny houses are trendy, and anything trendy is usually backed by people looking to make a quick buck.

- Tiny houses are incredibly expensive for their size. Their prices frequently range from $450 to $650 per square foot. In comparison, an average custom-built house is in the $100 to $200 per square foot range, typically with the land included (although this does vary from area to area, of course).

- Tiny houses have to be inspected and registered by your local motor vehicle division, meaning you must pay ongoing, yearly registration costs.

- A tiny home will typically have higher insurance premiums than an RV.

- Tiny houses are very heavy, usually over 10,000 pounds. In comparison, my traditional travel trailer weighs a little over 5,000 pounds.

- They can be dangerous to move because they tend to be very top-heavy.

- They usually lack plumbing. If you want standard RV-style plumbing, it usually comes with an upcharge.

- They are usually made primarily of wood and are thus a fire hazard compared to RVs.

- Numerous counties will not allow you to use it as a permanent dwelling, thus at times you are not allowed to live in a mobile tiny home on your property.

I went to one of the more popular mobile tiny home manufacturer websites and priced out one that was around the same size as my current travel trailer. It came out to almost $80,000! I purchased my travel trailer brand new for $25,500. Don't get me wrong, the tiny home trailer was made from nicer materials, but it had no more functionality than my travel trailer. Unless you plan to move your dwelling once it is on location, a good alternative to the mobile tiny home is a regular house constructed just like a normal residence, only smaller.

I have lived in a "tiny home" by this definition—I called it a cottage—and I really enjoyed the simplified living. I originally thought about going this route when building my off-the-grid house, but I decided to go bigger. The main reason is that my off-grid home is still an investment. If I built a very small house, should I ever decide to (or had to) sell the property, the pool of prospective buyers would be drastically narrowed. Like many off-gridders, I plan to live in my off-grid property long term. However, unplanned events can happen in life, and I would rather build a house that is easier to sell should I need to.

Tiny homes have also become very trendy. With anything trendy, you should be prepared for those aforementioned bad contractors that prey upon the naïve by charging extra money for what's popular. I have heard unscrupulous contractors repeat a specific, unfortunate phrase time and again. . . .

"Smaller means more expensive."

No, it doesn't, actually.

In some parts of the construction process, yes, smaller does mean more expensive, because there is a fixed cost to the "starter" elements needed for a construction job. For example, the price of bringing heavy machinery to a remote site or the cost of permits will be the same whether the job is small or massive. This type of fee will obviously increase the average cost per square foot for your house relative to a larger project.

Now, in the big picture these costs should not add a drastic amount to your total fee, but guess what good old Joe Six-Pack (the incompetent contractor) does? He charges up (adds unjustifiable fees) to a smaller project . . . not because it costs more. He does this because he wants to make a killing for doing less work. I have been quoted these kinds of inflated prices by contractors and witnessed contractors doubling or tripling the cost for small projects.

I'll be honest; it can be difficult to even find a contractor willing to do a small project unless they can charge inflated prices. In their mind it just isn't worth it to do the project for a reasonable fee. That makes sense for a big-time busy contractor. But for your small community everyday contractor, this is a terrible business move. Contractors who bid like this usually go belly up when the economy trends down because they refused to stay busy with big *and* small projects alike.

Sure, when buying certain building supplies in a larger quantity, you can get a discount. But you should not pay three times more per square foot for a smaller house than you would pay on a larger project.

So what's the solution? If you decide to go tiny, make sure that your tiny house is built at a fair cost. Consider purchasing an off-the-shelf set of tiny home building plans and getting the materials yourself. Then have your contractor bid on labor only, with a "not to exceed more than" clause in the job contract. Any contractor worth their salt will have no problem doing this, as it makes their life a lot easier. Instead, they have someone else put together the building plans and get building materials. This way, all they have to do is show up and build, while you are the gofer who gets whatever they need. Also, most builders/contractors love the building side of things. So it could be a motivator to get someone who would not regularly take on such a project.

If you don't have a truck or can't get the supplies yourself, ask if your building supply company will deliver them directly to your site. Ask what additional fees this might add. A good set of tiny house plans will actually have a materials list which you can send to your building supply company. This is called a "building package". Also consider how you will store the supplies at your site (preferably in a secure, weather-proof location such as a shed or lockable trailer). If you leave them out in the elements, they could get ruined or stolen before you have the chance to use them.

For some off-gridders, the delivery method mentioned above may not be an option. Remember building remotely means delivery might not be possible because of distance, driveways that are poor and/or inaccessible to big vehicles, road conditions, etc. This happened in my case—almost all the materials for my project (except concrete, more on this in a bit) had to be hand-carried. On one job, we ended up having to get a bulldozer to drag the cement truck up to my building site. This created two problems. First, we could only fill the truck up halfway (to keep it at a good towing weight), so I had to pay double the price for my concrete. Second, the first truckload was almost full and about killed the (very expensive) bulldozer and tore the crap out of the concrete truck. It was so bad those contractors have never called me back, even though I've called them with several job opportunities. Since then, all my cement had to be mixed with a small mixer or in a wheelbarrow and poured out by hand. Are you starting to see why your roads are an important part of your property hunt?

Remember to carefully track the money you spend on building supplies. This is called a "bill of materials" in contractor-speak and should include the cost of labor for building your home. Depending on your circumstances, this may impact the capital gains taxes you owe when you eventually sell.

Finally, make sure you can return excess or unused supplies or items to the store. When building remotely, it is better to have extra than not enough. I always try and buy more supplies than I need. Believe me, those trips for a bag of screws or a couple more pieces of lumber add up. I usually wait until I'm done with a certain phase of my project before I take back the extra or unneeded supplies. You never know what and how much you need until the project is close to done.

Of course, some good contractors will charge fairly for a tiny home project. But it usually takes more time and effort to find these contractors. Those I have found are usually into the off-the-grid or simple-living lifestyle themselves. Remember an off-the-grid building project is already a non-typical project. Throw in a tiny home on top of that, and you're making it even more unusual. Hard to find the right talent when you're taking the road less traveled.

Now, if you plan to build a tiny house on your own, it will cost you far less. The odds of you recovering your initial investment will be far higher. Even with greatly narrowing the potential home-buying demographic by building a tiny house rather than a regular house. I know people who built a standard stick-built tiny home for around $35 to $50 a square foot. That's about a third to a quarter what you will pay for today's new construction home in 2020.

You can save even more by doing all of the work yourself—especially if you use materials from your own land. I will warn you though; this is not as easy as it sounds. Otherwise everyone would be doing it. If you have ever tried to mill your own lumber from a log or splice your own hand-split wooden shingles in your backyard, you know what I'm talking about. However, building a tiny home from the resources on your own land is doable, especially if you're handy and have a lot of time to devote to the project.

CHAPTER 9

Off-The-Grid Power

UNDERSTANDING SOLAR, WIND, HYDRO, AND GEOTHERMAL ENERGY OPTIONS

A Brief History

Humans have been using sun, wind, and water as sources of free, clean power for thousands of years. Sailboats, sundials, and dams are long-used examples of how natural energy sources have been—and in many cases still are—being used. Throughout mankind's history and still today, there are entrepreneurs, politicians and others who have figured out how to sell and regulate something that is free.

Here's a perfect example of just how powerful the Sun is. Every day, the Sun produces 35,000 times the amount of the total energy required for *everyone* who uses electricity! Plus, sunlight is 100 percent free and natural.

There is no better way to become self-sufficient than to take advantage of natural and unlimited power sources. Sure, natural energy might not be as efficient as our modern power grid. But they are a great way to take a step away from the grip of the Gridmasters in government and the corporate world. It's a loophole around government regulations and the increasingly tightening grip of privatized utility companies. I'll tell you first-hand there is nothing better than saying goodbye to monthly utility bills.

It's also empowering to be in control of your own energy source. Especially when *you* control how and when you use it. I still remember my water utility company in Southern California forcing residents to conserve water due to an ongoing drought. The residents did such a good job conserving water the water company raised everyone's rates, because of unexpected lower revenues . . . I kid you not! For me, this was one of the straws that broke the camel's back. It's one of many reasons I left California for a lifestyle that wasn't controlled by bureaucrats.

An Introduction to Alternative Power Systems

When it comes to living off-the-grid, there are many challenges. Probably the most critical (after access to water) is the question of how to manufacture your own power (electricity) for your off-the-grid property.

By definition, "off-the-grid" means not being tied to any type of public utility. Of course, you could still use an alternative power source while tied to the grid. But that is not complete off-the-grid living. There is nothing wrong with this lifestyle. Actually, a lot more people in residential neighborhoods are taking advantage of alternative energy options. That said, you can still use one or more alternative power sources even if you do not plan to live 100 percent off-the-grid.

Of course, there are reasons to stay connected to the grid. For example, you may have essential medical equipment that requires a consistent energy source. It all depends on your goals, your land, and your budget.

Prior to my off-grid adventure, all my previous homes were tied to the grid, and I had never used an alternative or green power source. Needless to say, I had to start from scratch and figure out what the best avenue of alternative power was for my needs. Not to mention, I had a hard time finding other people who were using alternative power sources. So, I couldn't ask anyone I knew for feedback.

My hope is that this section will answer a lot of questions about living off-the-grid when it comes to your energy source. The most effective and reliable system is one that incorporates all three of the primary alternative power systems—solar, wind, and water. These three energy sources complement each other since they work in varying weather conditions (more on this later). This threefold combination might not be practical for most people. For example, if you don't have access to a stream for a hydro power solution, water-driven power is out. Usually, two of these three power sources can be utilized by most off-gridders. It depends on your specific property type and location. This is another reason you should have your goals and research taken care of before looking for land!

Before we get started, this section is not meant to be highly technical or to provide you with template systems. Remember, self-reliance is necessary for going off-the-grid. My goal is to inform you about the most common alternative power sources and how they work. There are many books offering detailed information about how to set up these systems from A to Z. I'm no expert in this area, and detailed explanations are better left to the professionals who do this on a daily basis. Not to mention the technology is changing very rapidly. Again, my goal is to help you help yourself in getting these energy sources working for you.

Since I brought up professionals, you should know that alternative energy systems offer a rare opportunity for a tax credit. I'm talking about a dollar-for-dollar reduction in the amount of income tax you owe. That's much better than a tax deduction! So, one professional you'll want to consult is an accountant.

If you'd like to know more about this, research the Residential Renewable Energy Tax Credit before you build. It could potentially save thousands of dollars on your green-energy-system building costs. Also, check out www.dsireusa.org for a nationwide listing of many other green-energy financial incentives, which vary by state, county, and local utility providers. Now, let's unpack these three natural energy systems one at a time.

Off-The-Grid Solar Power

What is solar power? Solar power is when the Sun's light or heat is converted into a usable energy source. Solar power is becoming increasingly popular and affordable. Just like the technology behind computers, solar technology keeps improving. This means it's becoming easier and more affordable to live an off-the-grid lifestyle—with many of the amenities we have become used to in the modern world using solar power. Matter of fact, as I write this, solar panels are more efficient and close to half the price they were when I first started my off-the-grid project.

The two most common uses of solar energy are the generation of heat and electricity. Solar power generates heat in the form of "solar hot water". That's what those black pipes you see on pool house rooftops do, they help to heat pool water. Today, a common use of solar energy is harnessing the Sun's rays into usable electricity—typically via a solar photovoltaic (PV) system. This is what those large black-glass panels you see on rooftops or mounted on special frames on the ground do.

Before we dive into some technical points, let me just say that we'll be focusing on true off-the-grid solar. That is, a stand-alone system consisting of the panel array, batteries, and a back-up generator which exists solely to provide power for your home.

Here's the important distinction: With off-grid solar, your solar panels generate energy which goes into your home and the extra is stored in your battery bank. With on-grid solar, you are essentially using the solar power to supplement your grid-tied power and selling your extra generated power to your power company. Here is the catch today: Because of the solar power boom in residential homes, a lot of utility companies are no longer allowing on-grid homes to sell their extra alternative energy produced power back to them. Oh, you have to love those greedy utility companies, they realized that buying back power generated by alternative energy systems was cutting into their bottom line.

Now, a whole bunch of "in-between" on/off-grid hybrid models and utility "buy-back" programs exist. But don't worry. We won't get in the weeds with the technical nuances of each one. For now it's crucial to understand that solar (particularly on-grid solar) is strongly regulated. This is done to ensure safety and consistency of on-grid energy from state-to-state, county-to-county, and even regionally—depending on which power company serves your area. So the rules that apply to your solar setup might not apply to a residential solar setup for someone living just five miles away from you. Still both on and off-grid solar setups are subject to local building codes and regulations.

I highly recommend you research your state, county, and utility provider's policies regarding solar before building. Particularly if you plan to have an on-grid component to your system. I will tell you this, my system is the only (or at least one of the only) fully approved solar systems in my county. I went through several phases to include inspections to gain this approval.

Now, for many readers, the first question will be . . .

"Will we get enough sun at our home to take advantage of solar power?"

That will depend, again, on where you live. Here is a great tool to estimate the amount of usable sunlight per day in your area:

https://pvwatts.nrel.gov

Disclaimer of the above website: The original website destination has changed numerous times since I first published this book. At the writing of this, late 2020, the above website is the latest version to figure out your usable solar energy in your area. You will have to do a little digging as the links to this information seem to be moving on a regular basis. This is the main website that should get you going in the right direction.

In addition, I have developed a simple way to estimate (with emphasis on estimate) how much sun power you might be able to generate per day using a solar panel system.

Solar panels combined maximum watt output ×
average hours of sunlight/day × 0.5 = daily sun power generated

Note: In this equation, 0.5 is used as an estimate of power loss due to system inefficiencies and conversion factors.

For example, my system at this time consists of (12) 300-watt solar panels. I have added panels over the years and some are 300 watts while others are a little more, but I like round numbers. This gives me an estimated maximum watt output per/hour of 3,600 watts. To convert watts to kilowatts, simply divide your watts by 1,000:

3,600 watts ÷ 1,000 = 3.6 kilowatts (kW)

According to the latest information using the above website, the average sunlight per day in my region is 4.5 hours.

So our equation will look like this:

$$3{,}600 \text{ watts} \times 4.5 \times 0.5 = 8{,}100 \text{ watts of}$$
average power produced per day (or close to 8 kilowatts per day)

This is more than enough power for my daily power use. How can you know what your daily power usage will be? In an off-grid situation, the only way to calculate this is to list every power-using item you have (or intend to have) and add them up. Now, this method is not an exact science, but it will give you an idea of how big your system should be. Here is the key point to take away—your solar power system will change and grow. Always overbuild it, instead of underbuilding it. It is far more expensive to replace pieces to your system that are too small than it is to spend a little more up front. Today, solar panels are fairly cheap. Trust me I have almost doubled the original number of solar panels I started with, which is common for most off-gridders.

If you are converting an on-grid home to off-grid power, it is much easier. Just look at your average monthly consumption over the last twelve months (bearing in mind you will probably use more power at certain times of the year). In case you don't know where to find this, it's right on your monthly power bill.

Gary's Simple System and Recommendations

When I first planned my off-grid home, I was not a solar technology expert by any stretch. I had to learn on my own. I soon found that trying to learn every aspect of developing my own solar power system (from scratch) was a task better left to professionals. I'm not saying you can't do it yourself. I'm just saying that for me, it was better to learn the basics and then work with someone who could recommend a system. Once I'd picked my system, I could find a certified electrician to help do the installation.

Again, don't let me discourage you. Many people with no experience have put in their own solar systems in off-grid houses. Again, this was about how much I felt I could learn and tackle at the time. There are many things going on during an off-grid home project. So you have to pick and choose how much time and resources you are willing to invest in each one. Would I still be willing to tackle this same project on my own today? Maybe, maybe not, but I definitely have a better understanding of solar and alternative power. I've also made most of the upgrades and changes to my system myself since it was first installed.

For my installation, I used a company close to where I live called *Backwoods Solar*. They have been in the alternative energy business for over twenty years, and they have it down pat.

Today, there are numerous alternative energy companies who do something very similar to *Backwoods Solar*. It is best to use someone close to your area if you can. This way you can go and pick up the parts you need in person, and ask any questions you may have. I don't like purchasing most alternative energy components online, but that is just me.

I did this because, when it comes to home building, there are certain things I can do well or which I can quickly learn. However, the potential risk and liabilities of hooking up a power-generating electrical system to my own home was just not worth it. If I screwed something up installing the solar system myself, it might have cost thousands of dollars to either replace the damaged equipment or to hire a professional to redo the job.

So, unless you have extensive building experience, installing your own solar array can be very unsafe. (It's live electricity, folks!) I'm all for learning new things, but I'm also a pragmatist. I know there are professional fields for a reason. I would rather save myself the stress and buy some peace of mind by paying for skilled help.

Nevertheless, for my own solar array, I did all the non-electrical grunt work myself. This saves cash, and lets you be as independent as possible in setting up your off-grid home. For my project, I purchased and organized all the equipment at the building site, readying it for installation. I also mounted all the solar panels (i.e. attached them to their metal racking base), and roughed in all the mounting for the other components (such as the inverter—a big metal box of electrical components that needs to be installed, too).

Then, I left all the hookup and electrical work for the electrician. Not only did I save thousands of dollars, I had the reassurance it would be installed correctly.

Basic Solar Power System Components

A solar electric system is made up of much more than just a bunch of black panels. Here are the other components you will need for building a complete system.

SOLAR MODULES: Panels are installed in groups of 1 to 18+ modules on a solar mount, which in turn attaches to a building, to the roof of an RV, or atop a metal post or racks in the yard. Together, this is called your "Solar Array". Each solar module is wired to the other modules in the array by sunlight-tolerant solar interconnect wiring. Several arrays may be wired to a solar combiner box, where they are all connected to heavier underground wires which transport the power to your battery and equipment room (explained below).

A CHARGE CONTROLLER: This is a small wall-mounted piece of electrical equipment. Your charge controller receives power from solar, wind, or micro-hydro generators, and controls the flow of power to the batteries. When the batteries become full, the charge control automatically cuts back, stops, or diverts the charge. This prevents overcharging, which would otherwise lead to battery damage. Your charge control may have manual control switches and lights or meters which will show your battery's charging status.

BATTERIES: These receive and store your DC produced electrical energy so they can be used when alternative energy devices are not producing power (i.e. no sunlight, no wind, no seasonal stream). Your batteries also instantly supply large surges of stored electricity in case you need them to run heavy power appliances which your solar panels or hydroelectric generator could not power by themselves. You should choose your batteries and battery bank size based on their power requirements and the mount of reserve power you might need. At the time I write this, battery technology is changing rapidly. Today you can choose a couple different types of storage batteries. The two most common are:

Option 1—Lead Acid Batteries: Lead acid batteries are a long-standing technology that has been used in off-grid energy systems for decades. While they have a relatively short life span (7-10 years depending on use and care) they are also one of the least expensive options. A bank of lead acid batteries can weigh from a couple hundred pounds (just 1 or 2 batteries) to thousands of pounds. The electrolyte in lead acid batteries is highly toxic, can cause severe skin burns, and requires a venting system to mitigate off-gassing.

Option 2—Lithium Ion Batteries: Lithium ion batteries are the new technology on the block. When they first hit the market, they were cost-prohibitive for most off-gridders. But they are becoming more affordable and are now considered the "go-to" replacement for lead acid batteries if they fit into your budget. Lithium ion batteries are lighter and more compact than lead acid batteries. They also have a longer lifespan when compared to lead acid batteries. You can have a fully functional backup battery system that weighs less than a hundred pounds, which will last 20-40 years, and take up a fraction of the space lead acid batteries might take up. The downside is that they cost more.

POWER INVERTER: The major electronic component of a power system, it converts DC power stored in batteries to 120-volt AC—which is standard household power. Short, heavy cables with a large fuse or circuit breaker carry battery power to the inverter. After conversion to AC, power from the inverter usually connects into the circuit breaker box of your house, in place of your utility lines. The house breaker box routes power to lights, appliances, and outlets of your house. Inverters can range from a couple hundred watts to several thousand.

A system like mine that uses the above components costs about $10,000 to $15,000. This varies based on the type and number of your storage batteries.

Solar Power Limitations

Obviously, your biggest limitation with solar power is the amount of sunlight in your area. If you live in a place like Arizona or Southern California, you can probably get by using solar power alone. Especially if you have the right battery storage capacity for your energy needs in place.

In less sunny areas, you will need more than one alternative power system *and* good battery storage. This is because, when there is no sunlight (such as at night), you will need to utilize stored solar power or your other alternative power systems (wind, hydro etc.). The same goes for less sunny times of the year.

A good battery bank is also important because the Sun's light is not static. Meaning, it will not have full solar power all the time. Instead, it will vary based on the position of the Sun throughout the day. Since we're talking about batteries, you should know that they're currently the most finicky parts of an off-grid solar array. I'm talking in terms of their ongoing maintenance and replacement costs. I recommend carefully researching the pros and cons of different battery choices before making a decision about your off-grid solar array. The new lithium battery technology simplifies this greatly, but they do have limitations such as heat and cold tolerances, when compared to lead acid batteries.

Because the Sun moves across the sky throughout the day, there are solar panel mounting systems that can either be rotated manually or have small motors installed. These motors rotate your panels for maximum sunlight exposure. I did look into this option, but the cost and effort did not make sense. Solar panels are so cheap today; it is cheaper to add panels than to design an elaborate solar panel rotation system. That said, I have seen some pretty sophisticated automatic rotating solar panel systems that work really well. It just depends how much you are willing to spend.

A more effective solution is to install a complementary energy system to offset the limitations of sun power. For example, on a stormy, wet day, you won't get much sunlight and therefore not much solar electricity . . . but you may well have good wind or rain (hydro) options due to the turbulence and/or downpour! This makes wind power a good supplement to your solar array.

Off-The-Grid Wind Power

Generating "wind power" simply means using a wind turbine (propeller) to catch the wind and turn a turbine connected alternator or generator which can then produce electric power. Essentially, this system converts mechanical energy (the movement of the wind) into electrical energy.

For wind power, I suggest using a small wind turbine (6-foot diameter or smaller) to supplement your main off-grid power system. Larger turbines can put out a great deal of power today, but the cost and size are out of reach for most off-gridders.

With that said, smaller wind turbines have become incredibly affordable. Most come in under $1,000 (not including installation). Once you jump past the 6-foot-turbine size, the price moves up very quickly. As an example, you can get a wind turbine in the 6-foot diameter range for $1,000 or less; a turbine with a 15-foot rotor can start to get in the $10,000 range. I know what you're thinking . . .

"How much wind does it take to produce electricity?"

On average, a small wind turbine requires only a six to seven mile per hour wind to produce a usable amount of energy. For example, a small wind turbine can produce enough power daily to run a small energy-efficient electric refrigerator. All you need is a reasonable amount of consistent wind.

The good news is most regions in the United States have sufficient wintertime winds to support most off-grid power needs. To find the specifics for your area, use this winter wind guide:

http://www.primuswindpower.com/solarwind-solution/

Basic Wind Power System Components

The great thing about adding wind power to supplement your solar power system is that the components are almost the same. You simply tie your wind turbine into your solar power and battery storage system. The new wind turbines have smart technology, so they are already made to connect to most any solar array. Unless you're using a larger turbine, wind power systems are used to supplement your main power generating system.

Gary's Simple Wind Power Recommendations

My recommendation is to use a hybrid system of solar panels and wind power. This will work for most off-gridders. The primary source

of my off-grid electricity is my solar array. The primary reason I recommend a hybrid system is that you'll be leveraging nature's two
most accessible and reliable power sources—wind and sunlight.

My wind system ties directly into my solar power conversion
setup; and consists of one *Primus* 46-inch wind turbine. The thing
is, I'm not using my wind turbine as a means to supplement my
alternative energy system. I'm primarily using it to trickle charge
my batteries during the winter when I'm not at my off-the-grid
house. In cold weather, lead acid battery electrolyte can freeze
causing problems if the batteries do not maintain a 100 percent, or
close to 100 percent charge. There are numerous different ways
to remedy the problem of lead acid batteries freezing if you live in
your home all year around. For me it is just not worth it to install
and monitor these other solutions with me not being there, so using
a wind turbine is my solution.

Just how much electricity will this produce? When you consider
that, according to the U.S. Energy Information Administration, the
average American household uses about 30 kilowatts of power per
day; it might not seem like enough. But as an off-gridder, you're not
the average American.

Also, remember that my household at this time consists of one
human and two dogs. So, I can use a smaller system than most.
But I feel, with some conscious changes to your energy consumption habits, your off-grid households could make my system work.
Off-grid homes also typically use a number of energy efficient appliances, and have learned to eliminate energy-hogs (such as air condi-
tioners) or to at least run them on propane. As of now, in the summer
I'm cooling my house off a 12,000 BTU cooler. I started out with only
six solar panels, but now I have twelve and am running my cooler
all day. I could have run everything I had with just the first six, but
it was just not enough power in general. It's better to overbuild your
system from the start. Everyone I know starts with a basic system and
then builds onto it. This is because you don't know what your needs
are until you get out here. I soon realized that it's too hot in the summer to rely on only six solar panels and to keep my batteries charged,
while running my air conditioner. I also learned that you should have
solar panels that are moveable. You'll only need to move them during

the hot season—which, for us in Washington is two to four weeks of the year. Most of the year, you won't need to move your panels. But it still makes sense to have movable panels, instead of adding four new static ones, just to get the same result.

Limitations of Using Wind Power

One of the main problems with larger wind turbines, in addition to costs, is they make a lot of noise and take up a lot of space. Just imagine a 15-foot rotor somewhere on your property. It needs to be mounted up fairly high and is almost two stories tall! I don't know about you, but that is not very practical. Not to mention, at that size, their installation is not really a do-it-yourself project.

Wind also presents a consistency problem. It's just not always windy outside! In contrast, the Sun always shows up and emits energy, even when covered by clouds, smoke, or haze; it's just sometimes at a reduced rate.

In contrast, the wind is far less consistent, and there is no way to predict what amount of energy it will be able to produce from day to day. Moreover, the power output of a wind system can be affected by the topography surrounding your property. High objects (such as trees) surrounding it can also limit its wind exposure. This is why, for some off-gridders, hydro power makes more sense as a supplementary power source.

Off-The-Grid Hydro Power

If you already have an alternative energy (solar and/or wind) system, a micro-hydro setup can be a great supplementary power source. That is, provided you have a stream running through your property. The downside is that regulations for hydro power are changing all the time. So make sure it is permissible in your city and county. Two things I can pretty much guarantee: It will require a permit and your system will have to be inspected and approved. How much power can you produce using water? It depends on two factors:

1. *Flow* is the amount of water that flows past a given point in a given time period.

2. *Head* is the water pressure, or how hard the water flows past a given point.

Higher pressure, higher water volume, or a combination of both will increase your system's ability to produce sufficient power. A micro-hydro system essentially consists of a piece of pipe (the length will vary). These components capture flowing water (such as in a down-hill stream) and uses it to turn a turbine, thereby generating electricity.

Four questions will determine which micro-hydro system is right for you:

1. What is the elevation change (from intake to the turbine) over the length of the pipe?
2. How many gallons per minute of flow are there (minimum and maximum)?
3. What is the size, type, and length of pipe (if it's already installed)?
4. What is the wire distance from the hydro plant (lower end of creek) to the home or power-shed?

Just as with your wind turbine system, a hydro system can work off the same basic components as a solar array. Now, you don't need to have a solar system to use a hydro or wind turbine system. Just note that the battery storage and DC to AC conversion work off the same components and principles for each system.

That said, if you have consistent water flowing through your property, micro-hydro is a great way to go. Many people use sea-sonally flowing creeks to supplement their off-grid system—your choice will depend on your resources and needs. Of the three main alternative energy-producing sources, hydro is considered the most reliable and cheapest since water usually runs 24/7, 365 days a year. This makes a hydro system a continuous and cheap power source. This is why hydro is my number one recommendation for off-grid power—assuming you have access to it.

When I was first looking at properties, I considered some prop-erties with small streams running through them. I did this for two reasons:

- Easy access to water
- Generating power

In the end, I decided to purchase a property without a stream in exchange for one with a great view. I wake up seeing the sun rise over fog-wrapped mountain tops, bushy forests and an idyllic lake. I also made this decision for several practical reasons:

- In my area, more water means more bugs.
- Streams in my area can dry up at certain times of the year.
- Your power generating stream could be diverted away from your land by a property owner who lives higher upstream.

I did initially try going for the off-grid trifecta:

1. Isolated land
2. A great view
3. A hydro-worthy stream

However, this "perfect" situation was incredibly difficult to find, not to mention an expensive proposition where it did exist. In the end, topography, shade, water access, the height of surrounding structures, your budget, local permitting and regulations, and your personal goals in going off-grid will all impact which combination of alternative energy systems is best for you.

Off-The-Grid Geothermal Energy

'm not currently using geothermal power as part of my own off-grid experience. However, I wanted to include it as an option. If you have the right type of property and can afford it, geothermal is a great option.

Geothermal is the only energy source that comes from the Earth itself. It's usually used for heating and cooling. Thankfully, the technology has come a long way, and now it can be used to generate power as well. Of all the alternative energy sources, I find geothermal to be the most versatile and reliable of all. After all, the Earth's core isn't going to cool down anytime soon! If it does, we've got bigger things to worry about than having reliable power.

The core of the Earth is around 8,000 degrees Fahrenheit. The deeper you go toward the Earth's core, the hotter it gets. So, there is a great deal of potential free, constant energy directly under your feet. Geothermal energy originates from the inner mantle of the Earth as hot magma (liquid rock) circulates upward while surface groundwater seeps downward. The magma then heats the water and forces it back up through faults and cracks in the Earth's surface. When liquid forms, this geothermal energy is referred to as hydrothermal. The best part is that geothermal can be tapped into almost anywhere in the world! Because of this, areas with volcanic activity offer the best geothermal possibilities, while highly elevated and mountainous regions offer the poorest.

The complexity and type of any prospective geothermal system will depend on how your area fits into the above rating system. There are many variations of geothermal energy systems, but I will stick with the basics for now.

How a Geothermal System Works

As stated earlier, the primary use for geothermal energy is the heating and cooling of industrial buildings and residential homes. However, with advances in technology, it is now also possible to produce small amounts of electricity.

A geothermal setup sort of works like the solar pipe heating systems found on roofs that heat pools. Geothermal performs the same function, only it gets power from underground. This is an oversimplification of course, but it is pretty close. With geothermal energy, you are taking advantage of the consistent temperature of the Earth, harnessing it through an underground piping system and transporting it to the structure you wish to heat or cool. This piping system is called a "loop". The heart of a typical geothermal system is a ground-source heat pump that cycles water through this underground piping loop. This loop can be either an open or closed system loop.

CLOSED-LOOP SYSTEMS: This will circulate a water-based solution through a "loop system" of small-diameter, high-density polyethylene underground pipes. They can be installed horizontally, vertically or in a pond or river.

OPEN-LOOP SYSTEMS: This will use existing well water or surface water.

During the winter, geothermal heating and cooling systems absorb heat stored in the ground via the water that circulates in the underground loop. This heat is carried to the ground source heat pumps, where it's concentrated and sent as warm air throughout your home.

During the summer geothermal heating and cooling systems absorb heat from your home and transfer it to the underground loop, where it is absorbed by the cooler earth. The geothermal heat pump then uses this cool water returned from the ground to create cool, dehumidified air for your home. For a geothermal system to make usable electricity, steam must be produced and used to spin a turbine attached to a generator, which produces electricity. This is how traditional geothermal plants have produced energy for communities for decades.

Gary's Take on Geothermal Energy

As I indicated, I have no plans to use geothermal on my property. I did research this option early on and received a rough price quote for a system. For a complete, installed system, it was going to cost between $30,000 and $35,000, which is more than double the cost of my solar and wind system.

What my research indicated was that residential geothermal systems can produce electricity, but only in small amounts. So they are really not cost efficient as you will still need a different electricity system of some kind.

The biggest advantage of geothermal for people is that it makes it easier to power a modern central heating and cooling system. Another upside is that, once it is installed, there are very few additional costs. But because of the power that these systems typically use, they are usually not good options for off-the-grid living.

Now, if you are resourceful you can make your own affordable geothermal system using ABS or PVC piping. There are plenty of online forums on this topic. So if you have the time and patience, this could be a way to go. While the performance will not be as good as a professionally installed system, I have seen these systems work fairly well when done right. Most of these systems, however, are in hotter climates, such as Arizona.

The downside of a professionally installed system, of course, is the initial cost. Of all the alternative energy systems, I have found geothermal energy to be the most expensive. Still, it is also the most versatile and consistent of all the systems. Again, it all comes down to your budget and goals.

Generator Backup Systems

When I started my off-the-grid project, I knew very little about how backup generators fit into the equation. I'll tell you more about my rookie mistakes in a minute. For now, we will discuss the most common and basic backup generator systems.

Backup generators can run off any one of the following fuel types:

- Propane
- Natural gas
- Gasoline
- Diesel gasoline

For practicality and ease, the most popular free-standing generators run on gasoline. In contrast, your true backup residential generators usually run on propane or natural gas.

Type 1: Free-standing (Portable) Generators

DETAILS: These generators are fairly inexpensive and easy to find. The smaller ones can be hand carried, and the larger, heavier ones usually have wheels to help when moving them around. They typically range from 1,000 to 10,000 watts of peak power output. The cost of a generator can range from $200 to $1,000 for an 800 to 8,000 watt unit (0.8kW to 8kW). They come with a pull starter or a push-button starter.

PROS: Portable generators are cheaper and have a multitude of uses because they are mobile.

CONS: They usually run on gasoline, may still require professional installation to ensure you don't damage your existing alternative energy system(s), will have to be hand-started to charge batteries or provide additional power to your house, and they can be very loud.

Type 2: Mounted (Residential) Backup Generator

DETAILS: These generators are what you will see in electrically insecure areas. For instance, some neighborhoods in Florida are prone to frequent power outages from seasonal storms. These generators are permanently mounted on a concrete slab and will run off natural gas or propane. These are almost always automatic. This means they kick on automatically once the power goes out, or when your battery storage level has hit a predetermined point.

It's important to note that these types of generators are used differently in an off-grid home, compared to typical on-grid residential properties. Each type of generator will be virtually identical in appearance but the set-up is totally different. For an off-grid property, mounted backup generators are typically set-up to start when your batteries drop below 50 percent of their charge, or another predetermined charge level, usually 60 percent. (We'll discuss why this is important to battery life in a moment.) This "start-up" level is programmed into the system.

You can also have them kick in when you use more power than your alternative energy system will provide. For instance, if you want to have all the electric appliances and creature comforts of a standard grid-tied residential home regardless of the capacity of your off-grid energy system.

PROS: These days, you can build a very large and complex alternative energy system that can power almost any lifestyle you want, but it is cost prohibitive for most. For those who don't want to give up the creature comforts typical of grid-tied homes, a simpler and much cheaper alternative is a hybrid alternative energy system with a residential backup generator. So the upside is that these generator types kick in automatically and are far more quiet than a portable gas generator.

CONS: These residential backup generators don't come cheap. Per my research, on average they range from $2,000 to $4,000 for a 10,000- to 20,000-watt unit (10kW–20kW), not including installation.

So, the downsides are cost, necessity of professional installation, and the fact that most manufacturers will not honor the warranty for off-grid use. This means you'll need a permit and inspection for proper installation, along with a large propane storage tank for a fuel supply.

Gary's Simple Backup System Recommendations

When I first started exploring an off-grid lifestyle, I thought I could just use alternative energy sources alone. But, sometimes my simple thinking gets me in trouble.

I didn't realize that going off-the-grid would require some type of backup power generator. I know what you are thinking; why the heck would you have to have a backup generator if you had a good alternative energy system? This is typical if you're used to waiting for the power company to "turn things back on", which usually happens within a few hours at most while in the city. But, while living off-the-grid you don't want to get caught without a backup power source.

- First, because my county requires me to have one by code.
- Second, stuff happens, and not having one is a bad idea.

Even while generating your own power, your system will not run perfectly all the time. For example, some cloudy weather with little or no wind for a couple of days means insufficient power for my needs.

A perfect example was when my inverter had a defect and I had to disassemble it, and ship it off to the manufacturer. Luckily this happened just as I was getting ready to leave my property for the winter. Without a backup generator to charge batteries and run my necessary home items, such as my refrigerator, I would have been dead in the water.

Moreover, the batteries today are limited in what they can do. If you drain them below 50 percent of their storage capacity on a regular basis, their longevity will diminish. That's why I recommend you use a generator to start charging them as they approach 50 percent charge capacity.

Plus, batteries are really expensive to replace and will last far fewer years than almost all other components of your alternative energy system. Make sure to factor battery replacements into the lifetime cost of owning an off-grid alternative energy system. Otherwise, you will have a nasty surprise when they stop working well after a few years! Your battery's lifespans will depend on the technology you choose, how you maintain them, and how often you are willing to (foolishly!) drain them to less than half of their charge.

Now back to my embarrassing novice missteps. I assumed I could run my property using only a small portable generator which I had previously used to power my electric tools. But for off-grid living, you need a bigger power source. I learned this the hard way.

Another issue surfaced when I needed to power my well pump before my solar array was up and running. Remember, even if you do not yet live at your building site, you may need water for things like mixing concrete. So, unless you want to rent a water truck or haul all your water for your needs, a pump comes in handy! Thus it turned out that I would need a generator with enough power to run the pump *and* have a 220-volt outlet.

Instead of wasting money on two generators, I decided to purchase a larger mobile generator. I ended up getting a really good deal from Costco (no this is not an endorsement for Costco) on a Westinghouse 7,000-watt gas generator. It was on sale for $599 with only $50 for shipping. By purchasing this larger generator, I killed two birds with one stone, and saved money doing it. Matter of fact I still own and use this as my primary backup generator. So, it has more than paid for itself. Now, some of you may be thinking . . .

"I can always buy a used generator."

However, I recommend getting a new one if it is in the budget. Your generator is going to get a lot of use—especially in the beginning—so it is well worth the money. When it comes to used generators, you never know what you are going to get or how many actual hours of use it has from its previous owner(s). Thus, second-hand generators are not always the bargain they appear to be. Yet, again, I never want to discourage anyone from saving and getting a deal. Just saying that a new generator might make more sense.

Here's another caveat. The more power output you need, the heavier your generator will need to be. So make sure you take that into consideration. This is especially important if you plan to use it all over your property (when running power tools to construct an outbuilding, for example). With a full tank of gas, my generator weighs around 200 pounds, so unless you are one serious badass and lift trees with one arm, you'll need to consider the weight of your generator. Mine does have wheels, but moving it in the dirt and getting up ramps or a slope takes some serious effort. If I need to move it to another location, there's no way I'm getting it into my truck without a ramp or crane.

This is why I also own a smaller, portable, and more quiet generator. This is the generator I use for my power tools and outdoor projects where I need a more portable option. Not only is it lighter and easier to maneuver, it uses far less gas than my larger backup generator. Between using less gas, being easier to maneuver, and putting fewer hours on my main generator, my secondary generator is well worth it.

Propane: An Off-Gridder's Best Friend

When I first began to think of going off-the-grid, with my mind in typical Gary-land, I initially thought I could get around using any type of "paid-for" energy source on my off-grid property. That was my original vision that once I went off grid, I'd never have to pay for power again. Wow, was I in for a slap-in-the-face reality check. I even thought I could get by without using propane-powered appliances. This sounded great on paper, but turned out to be a definite pipe dream.

Here is the main factor I didn't understand prior to construction of my house: The building code for my county required my home to have a reliable heat source on each floor.

This meant having a wood stove for heat wasn't going to cut it, I would need a non-portable heat-producing stove or heating unit—one which operated on a reliable energy source . . . thus, propane. Oops, didn't see that coming! Obviously, I'm living in a much colder part of the country (remember, I'm up in Washington state), so the county was making sure I didn't do something stupid, like freeze to death! I know it seems a little invasive to force someone to install a permanent propane-fueled heating source, but those are the rules. In the end, the permitting rules proved to be redundant because I would need a large propane tank to run other devices and appliances in the house anyway. Here's why:

- An electric water heater, or even an electric tank-less water heater was not an option since I wanted to rely on off-grid power generation. Now, if you have a zillion dollars and can afford your own super-huge private solar farm, this won't be an issue. But for us mere mortals working within normal means, we need to think about conserving electricity. So, if I wanted warm showers, I would need to install a propane fueled tank-less water heater.

- As stated above, I would need propane to run a permanently installed heating system so I could meet county building code requirements.

- An electric oven draws too much power, so I would need to install a propane oven.

- When it comes time to install a large backup generator, I'd also need a propane source tank to provide fuel for my generator.

As you can see, it is hard to get by without a propane fuel source when living off-the-grid. It can be done, but it is extremely difficult, especially if you are doing everything according to your city/county building codes.

Here's another propane-related tip. Initially in the beginning if you don't have the financial resources to install an adequate alternative energy system, (such as solar) consider that there is an entire market for off-grid, propane-powered appliances. I'm talking about refrigerators, freezers, heaters, stoves, and so on. They tend to be quite a bit more expensive than traditional electric appliances. But they are designed to either draw no electricity or to use standard alkaline batteries as an electrical power source, such as the igniter for a gas stove.

Incidentally, this is how travel trailers are set up. Most appliances in my travel trailer run off propane or electricity. In fact, if you want to experiment with off-grid living I highly recommend living in a travel trailer first, as they are set up quite like an off-grid house.

For most of you, I recommend installing a decent sized propane storage tank. If that's not possible, at least get some decently sized portable propane containers. In rural places, most propane delivery companies are accustomed to supplying rough, remote places. So you should be able to get propane delivered, no problem. Well, that's true during the warm and non-rainy months. When the weather gets bad or winter comes, you probably won't be able to get propane delivered. That is, unless your roads are well maintained. This is something else to consider when deciding on how much storage capacity you will need for your tank(s)!

Why You Need a Power Shed

A power shed is exactly what it sounds like: a shed that will house all of your alternative energy components, as I listed earlier. Here are the benefits of using a power shed:

- It can act as both a power shed and storage shed.
- Depending on size, it usually does not require a building permit (this will vary between states and counties).
- The power inverter is a bit noisy (it buzzes while power is being inverted for use). Having a power shed means keeping it away from your house where you won't be bothered by ambient noise.
- Lead-acid type batteries off-gas hydrogen and oxygen when being charged or discharged. Due to this, building codes in many places may require proper ventilation. So it's just easier and safer to keep them away from your primary living quarters.
- You can use the power shed as a template for your primary living structure.
- You can use it as a ready-made structure upon which to mount solar panels. (Caution: if this is your plan, make sure to build a roof that has southern exposure, which can withstand the weight

of the panels and racking, and which is away from any shade-creating structures—such as trees.)

For me, building a power shed was a great way to start my project. It gave me a place to store tools and other items, while I continued working on the property. Trust me, if you leave tools outside—or anything of value outside—someone will gladly come by and remove them for you. Living remotely doesn't mean no one knows you are there. In small communities, everyone knows what you are up to, especially thieves. So building a power shed is a great way to protect your belongings and your alternative energy equipment.

I also used it to experiment with different types of siding, roofing and paint color palettes for my house. You might want to try this yourself. After all, it is a heck of a lot cheaper and easier to change things on a shed than on a house, if you don't like them.

Be Careful When Hiring Electricians

Be careful when selecting an electrician for an off-the-grid project. A lot of them will tell you they are familiar with installing alternative energy systems when they actually have never done it before. In other words, they obviously just want the job. This happened with the first electrician I spoke to. However, the more I described my plan, the clearer it became that he had no clue how to do it. Needless to say, he fully intended to charge me for his learning curve. This is not to say a good electrician can't figure it out many certainly can—but a good one will not charge you so he can put in extra hours learning to install alternative energy systems. Thankfully, I eventually found an electrician who had installed a couple systems and who knew the basics of getting the job done.

Even though solar and other alternative energy systems are becoming more popular, I quickly learned that they're usually not entirely off-grid. They are typically grid-tied (connected in some way to the public utility grid) or have grid-tied components. We off-gridders are still a unique breed. So you will have to get a lot of the information about these systems on your own. The good news is, numerous off-grid focused alternative energy companies are a huge help in getting you on track and going in the right direction.

Putting It All Together

As you can see, there is a lot to think about when it comes to putting together an alternative energy system. The technology already exists to help you enjoy all the on-grid comforts you're used to. It can, however be very costly. Most of us will need to pick and choose which energy-consuming devices are truly necessary, and which we can live without. This way, we can all tailor our system(s) to fit our needs and desires.

The perfect system would combine solar, wind, hydro, and geothermal. Hey, I think unicorns are really cool too, but I'm not planning on seeing or riding such a mythological creature during my lifetime. The bottom line is: If we could each afford the perfect alternative energy system (and each lived on a property with the natural resources required for all four systems) our lives would be a lot easier. But that's not happening any time soon.

Instead, we can all learn to give ourselves a bit more (or a lot more!) while, at times, being less reliant on technology. Of course, this aforementioned dream system will not be affordable for the average person, even when it does become available. But who knows when that will even happen.

I think alternative energy systems are the most challenging part of creating an off-grid lifestyle. I hope this section gave you some clarity so you can decide which system (or combination of systems) is best for you.

I know when I first started my research, finding simple and straightforward information on the subject was like trying to find a needle in a haystack. There were plenty of books describing the engineering of alternative energy systems. They were replete with highly technical and difficult-to-understand information, but low on direction about choosing the best system. I hope this chapter has helped remedy that problem.

Final Thoughts

How to Live More Energy Efficient

In the beginning of this book, I talked about how living The Simple Life is a perfect way to start preparing for off-grid living. Case in point, when going off-the-grid, one of the biggest challenges will be using less energy than you used while living on-the-grid. It can also be hard to be continually aware of monitoring your energy use.

The size of your off-grid energy system and its capacity to store energy will determine the type and size of home appliances you can use. The more money you spend on your energy systems, the more everyday appliances you can have and use. Some systems are large and produce a great deal of electricity, so you wouldn't know the house is even off-the-grid. You've seen those "off-grid" houses on TV where the solar array and the engines that auto adjust it are six figure setups. That doesn't include the inverters and batteries. With enough alternative energy, you can power anything. But you don't want to go off-the-grid just to get back into the Cult of Clutter by overbuilding your house or energy systems. I run my entire house from 8:30 a.m. to 8:30 p.m., while often doing two loads of laundry and running the AC. I then reduce the use of energy hogging appliances, because now I'm running off the stored power in my battery bank. So, believe me, you don't need a nuclear power plant sized system to do this. But for most of us, this type of super-system, which runs into the six-figure range, will be cost prohibitive. You can solve this problem by simply changing our energy-use expectations by using fewer, or more efficient appliances.

Some of the electrical devices you use on a regular basis may be impractical once you have an off-grid power-generating system.

These are the appliances I recommend you think about if you need them or not:

- Forced heat and/or air conditioning
- Microwave
- Dishwasher (not always; they are becoming more energy efficient)
- Full-size (large) electric refrigerator (use a small one instead)
- Free-standing electric freezer
- Hair dryers
- Space heaters
- Portable air conditioning
- Electric stove/oven

- Electric water heater (I have never met an off-gridder who uses an electric water heater, they all use gas water heaters and most are tankless.)

- Electric clothes drier (I use a stackable washer/dryer unit, the washer is electric and the dryer is gas.)

As I have said, if you are willing to spend more money on your off-the-grid system, (usually in the $25,000 to $50,000 range), you can probably use most of the appliances you are accustomed to enjoying.

This applies to anyone using the three alternative power sources we just covered: solar, wind, and hydro. Geothermal is a different, and much more expensive type of system, and not an option for most. If you can afford it, however, some appliances on this list may be possible for you to have and use.

Again, this is not an all-inclusive list, but I have found these to be the biggest and easiest energy tips to follow.

- Use propane-powered appliances, where it makes sense.
- Hang-dry clothes during warm months.
- Install LED lighting throughout entire house.
- Install windows for maximum natural lighting. (This is known as "daylighting".)
- Install skylights for additional natural lighting.
- Turn lights off when you are not using them.
- Get the smallest and most energy-efficient refrigerator you can live with (this represents the biggest and most continuous power draw in an off-the-grid house).
- If you are building an off-grid property from scratch, consider using a passive solar home design. This will help you collect, store, and distribute the Sun's natural heat throughout your home in the winter and help reject it during the summer.
- Make sure your home is properly insulated.

For almost all of us, this energy-saving-lifestyle change will necessitate a big change in habits. However, with some energy-use reprogramming, you will soon wonder how you wasted so much power in the past.

Off-The-Grid Internet and Phone Access

H aving phone or internet access might not be that important for some off-gridders. Indeed, some folks go off-the-grid to get away from the noise of technology. However, I think for most of us having internet access and cell phone coverage is a must. Especially if you're running a remote business, which we'll talk about later. I've been working remotely since I've been off-the-grid. So, this was a crucial factor when selecting my property.

The first thing I checked when I initially looked at my property was whether it had cell phone coverage. Luckily the cell tower was directly across from my property on another mountain range, so I have excellent reception. For me, a property without cell phone coverage would be a deal breaker. This is especially important if you want some type of phone service and plan to live in an area without landline access.

Fortunately, today's ever-expanding cell phone coverage means there is a carrier in almost every area. At the very least, coverage is in your general area. So you may have to drive a bit to be within range. Yes, I do know people who do this to use their cell phone.

Bear in mind, unlike in the city, a remote area is likely to have one cell phone company with much better coverage (more towers) than the other major carriers. Ask a few locals who this company is, and whose calls drop the least when driving between tower ranges.

Here is another really good reason to have cell phone coverage on your off-the-grid property: emergencies. Living an off-the-grid lifestyle is inherently dangerous. With more freedom comes more risk. Not only are you farther away from your closest neighbors, you're also far from medical help. Due to the difficulty of my roads, were I to get severely injured, there would be no way for me to get medical help on my own. A neighbor or life flight would have to get me, and a cell phone would be my only way to raise the alarm.

So, in many situations, reliable cell phone service could literally be a matter of life and death. A cell phone signal booster (also known as a cell phone repeater) is a small electronic device that can help solve the problem of weak reception. The catch is you need some type of reception for it to work (in other words, it won't work in an area with no cell signal whatsoever).

While building my house, I lived in my travel trailer at a remote RV park that didn't have consistent cell phone coverage. Fortunately, I found a good booster that worked really well in low-level reception areas. The brand of booster I have and still use is called the *Wilson Electronics Vehicle Cellular Signal Booster*. Yes, it was designed for car use, but you can purchase the home adapter kit, and it works perfectly. I went from one bar of service, to between two to three bars of reception using this booster.

The downside is your phone has to stay in the cradle for it to work. The upside is it only cost around $100 bucks for the entire kit (other boosters can cost upwards of $400). I know a lot of people in the sticks who use this system, and for the money, it seems to work the best.

There are more expensive, and more powerful cellular boosters, but they require an internet router to work. Now, if you have internet access, this sounds great, but there is a catch. If you are living off-the-grid, you will not have hard-wired (underground cable) internet access. Instead, you will probably have to use a Wi-Fi cellular device or satellite internet. Unfortunately, these boosters will not work with this type of internet connection (more on satellite internet and how it works later).

It's also a good idea to have cell phone coverage for your remote security system. We will discuss off-grid security systems in detail in a later chapter. For now, it's important to note that some require cell service. For example, using game cameras that double as security cameras will require cell phone reception. This is how they send data directly to your phone, alerting you when there is movement on your property.

Sure, security systems can be operated with internet access instead of cell service, but this creates a reliability problem. This is because routers, connectivity, and power systems can go down, thus requiring a reboot of your internet equipment. If you are not at your property year-round, this could be a big problem. In contrast, I have found the cellular communication cameras to be the most reliable, which is another reason I recommend choosing a location with cell phone service.

Gary's Off-The-Grid Internet Access Solutions

Before going off-grid, I had become a bit "citified", when compared to my younger years. This meant I was used to constant high-speed internet access. Now, as you can guess, going remote and living off-the-grid changed this big time. Luckily, I had experimented with Wi-Fi mobile internet access for a couple years before fully committing to an off-grid lifestyle. So I knew I would need to spend time thinking about how to get off-grid internet access before buying land. But there was a problem with that solution too; the internet worked fine at my property. However, it didn't work at the RV park I was staying at during the construction of my house. My cell phone booster worked great for voice calls, but didn't work for data since it just had too much bandwidth (i.e. the signal was too "big" for the booster to handle).

This was a huge problem, as I need consistent internet access to run my business. So I had to explore other options. That is when I started looking at satellite internet companies. I remember back just a couple years ago hearing from people how slow and expensive satellite internet access was. Nevertheless, I contacted a couple of satellite internet providers and spoke with one of the local installers. This was how I learned that the technology has come a long way and is now a viable off-grid option.

Here is where my story got a little trickier. I soon discovered that satellite internet performance is inversely related to participation. Specifically, it's based on how many users are on the node in which you participate. A node is the electronic device that is attached to a network, and can create, receive, or transmit information over a communications channel. The more users on your node, the slower your service will usually be.

Here is how it worked for me. The first service I subscribed to is the biggest and most well-known satellite internet service provider in the United States, *HughesNet*. This is by no means an advertisement or promotion of their service; it is just to show you an example of my experience.

When I first subscribed with them, I had never used satellite internet. So I wasn't used to the lag time (the delay in connection speed). Still, my service seemed really slow. I thought I had an equipment problem. However, after discussing this with my installer, I learned that the node I was using on HughesNet was full, which was probably the reason my speeds were so slow.

Basically, a node only has so much bandwidth (capacity). So once that bandwidth gets used up, you will experience slow speeds. This was a huge problem, and a big pain in the butt for running my business. The bottom line was that it just wasn't going to work at the speeds and performance I was getting.

My installer said he would do some research and see if he could find a better solution. Fortunately, this kind of research usually comes without bias in a rural area. This is because, in more remote areas, installers are usually independent contractors and will typically perform installations for numerous satellite television and internet services. So, a local installer can give you the real story on each service without prejudice.

After asking around, my installer found another satellite internet service provider (called *Exede*), which had fewer people on the node for my area. At the time, I thought this was fantastic, although this feeling didn't last (more on this in a moment).

Here is another important point when it comes to satellite internet service providers: The installation is not free. By the time you factor in the equipment purchase or rental (I recommend renting the equipment), it is not cheap. Also, some will *not* give you a grace period to cancel. So it can be an incredibly painful experience if you are not happy with the service.

HughesNet did have a 30-day cancellation policy, so I was able to cancel my service without having to pay some ridiculous fee. That being said, I did lose my initial installation costs, which was in the neighborhood of $100. I also had to pay the installation cost of the new service. In total it cost me about $200 in fees, and believe me, these companies are not going to make an exception and reduce their fees. Trust me, I tried!

Even with the costs of changing services, it was a risk because Exede didn't have the same 30-day "try it out" grace period that HughesNet had. If I didn't like the service or it didn't work out, I was told I would have to pay a steep cancellation fee.

Here is where things got interesting with my satellite internet service. Exede worked great in the beginning. But then I started having serious problems. My connection kept dropping, and after many hours on the phone, and multiple service calls (at $90 a pop!), I finally cried uncle and gave up. No one could get it to work properly, so after I patiently explained my issues, they let me terminate my contract early without penalty. I was only a couple months from my house being livable. So I knew my Wi-Fi hotspot would work without all the headaches once I got settled in.

Overall, my experience with satellite internet service has been pretty crappy to be honest. Not to mention a huge waste of money and time. I have heard it go both ways, some people have no problems and then others, like me, have a ton of problems. If it is the only option and you are stuck, you will have to just live with the limitations of this type of service. Even now, as I'm writing the second edition of this book, nothing has changed with crappy satellite internet. It still sucks . . . and I have spoken with several users since then!

As I've mentioned, satellite internet has come a long way and is a better-than-nothing option if you don't have another choice. Nevertheless, it has some serious drawbacks when compared to cable or grid-tied internet services. Here is a list of the most noticeable issues I have found:

- Installation tends to be more expensive.
- There are fewer service providers.
- You need to have "line-of-sight" to the satellite for it to work. Your installer can help you determine if you have this or not.
- If you are in a part of the country that uses an old satellite, your service will more than likely be crappy.
- Bad weather such as clouds, rain, or snow, can and will knock your service out.
- There is limited data usage.
- You will have to be creative if you download or upload a lot of music or videos. While most companies have unlimited data usage times, they're usually available at times when you are asleep.
- You may have to pay for service calls if your service goes out for any reason.
- It requires an area upon which you can install a small dish (just like satellite TV).

Thankfully, you have a few alternative solutions for your internet, phone, and even TV.

Off-The-Grid Internet: WISP

A WISP (wireless internet service provider) is another option for off-gridders in certain areas. Unlike telephone or cable companies, a WISP does not need to run a physical cable to your location. This makes it ideal for rural and off-grid areas. Instead, WISPs use tower-mounted antennas to transmit and receive radio signals. So a WISP is similar to a cell service company in that it mounts its equipment (often onto a cell tower, water tower, or antenna). Its technology and type of service, however, are quite different.

To receive the WISP signals, you typically need a small dish mounted on your property. Satellite TV providers are similar to WISPs in that they deliver service to a fixed location that has a receiver dish. However, as with satellites, the signals must travel such long distances that lag can be a problem. In contrast, the signals from WISPs travel much shorter distances and are typically reliable, fast, and relatively cheap.

Here are the drawbacks. Most WISPS operate regionally, not nationally, so not all areas of the country have them. Like satellite internet, WISPs are negatively impacted by adverse weather. You will also need a clear line-of-sight to the tower or antenna from which the signal originates. This may mean cutting some trees and/or "bouncing" the signal off another structure and toward your home.

So, even if you are in the WISP service area, your home may not be able to take advantage of the service. However, if you can get WISP service, it's worth comparing the prices and reliability to satellite internet. As always, ask around with locals to determine what they have found works best.

Off-The-Grid TV: Satellite Television

Going off grid does not mean giving up TV for good. Although some people are happy to live without the dumb box, I know access is important for me. For one, I'm a sports fan (even though I watch sports far less than I used to). I also love educational shows on channels like Science, Discovery, National Geographic and The History Channel. Thankfully, there are solutions for getting your favorite shows while living off-the-grid.

Satellite television has been around a lot longer than satellite internet, so most people are familiar with the service. I sometimes used satellite TV instead of local cable services while I was still living on-the-grid. DISH Network and Direct TV are the two biggest satellite television providers in the United States. I have used both over the years. Which is right for you? It just depends on which types of channels and equipment you prefer. Although I have not heard of anyone not being able to get satellite TV service, I'm sure there are some exceptions. However, for most off-gridders, satellite television is a good option.

I actually have two dishes for my satellite TV services. I have a permanently mounted dish at my off-grid property, and another one that I mount to a portable tri-pod for use on the road. I simply take my main receiver and portable dish setup with me when I'm travelling to use with my trailer. There are small, portable dishes made for RV living now that automatically find the satellite for you.

I have used one of these as well, but they do have limitations. For one, they may have a lack of high-definition (HD) channels and no DVR capabilities.

A final thought for those who want to do part-year off-the-grid living like myself: All satellite television and internet service providers I currently use, and have researched, allow you to downgrade your services for six months out of the year. So instead of paying for a full subscription all year, you only pay a small fee and your equipment rental fees (if you do not own your equipment) for up to half a year. This is a great way to save cash if you only live at your off-grid property part time, and you are in a different area for some of the year.

Off-The-Grid Financing

A LITTLE CASH AND A LOT OF CREATIVITY

Now that you have your dream off-grid plan, you are going to need to pay for it. This means that—unless you are sitting on piles of cash—you will need to organize financing. Before you start on your off-grid journey I recommend reading my book *The Simple Life Guide to Financial Freedom*. There's also the question of how you're going to earn a living while off-the-grid, which we'll talk about in the final chapter of this book.

However, financing your off-grid project gets tricky. Probably the most valuable lesson I learned during this project was how incredibly difficult it is to finance an off-the-grid property using traditional financing tools.

Before I explain the interesting financial aspects of off-grid properties, I need to be clear: I'm not a financial expert, nor do I play one on TV. I'm only sharing the techniques used by myself and others to make this dream of a unique life adventure a reality. What I'll be sharing are examples only. Once you have your rough plans in place, it's best to speak to an actual tax and/or financing professional to make sure you have all your ducks in a row. Also, not all financial institutions will provide the same terms. So don't assume you can follow the same method without thoroughly researching all options available to you in your unique situation.

Here is how it played out in my case. When I first started the project, I thought things would play out as they did with past houses

I have owned or built. I thought I could get a construction loan or a traditional home loan. Not only was I wrong, I was *way* wrong with this assumption. I'm a debt free guy, so I was going to use the cash I had on hand, then finance the remainder to speed up the project. I was planning to pay off what I financed within a couple years of completing the project.

I soon found out that traditional institutions simply won't finance off-the-grid properties. I spent a great deal of time trying to find someone who would finance my off-grid home, and couldn't find any. After discussing my project with a particular lender specializing in VA loans, they indicated that banks would not finance houses that are not tied to public utilities, as they consider this type of property too risky an investment.

I found it interesting that banks had no problem financing people with hardly any earnings or job security during the housing boom, but turned up their noses at off-gridders. Back to the drawing board I went. The lender indicated if I were to run utilities to the property, even if I didn't intend to use them, I would be able to get traditional financing. So off I went to the public utilities division of my county, hoping there were utilities somewhere close to my property. It turned out that the closest utilities were over a mile away. In theory, this doesn't sound all that far, but when you are talking about running utilities in a rural area, that is a long way. I would have to pay privately to have them brought to my building site.

The quote for doing so came back at over $80,000! In addition, they wouldn't be able to run the cables underground. So it would all have to be done with above-ground power poles. The entire $80,000 would be due right away as well, since this type of project would have to be paid entirely up front, with cold hard cash, before the work even started. Ok, maybe not real cash bills, but you get the point. They were not going to lend me any money on promise of payment later. The risk appeared too high for them.

Even if I could poop out gold nuggets to pay for the utility run, I would have to get permission from every owner of the properties upon which the poles would be installed so that the utilities could reach my property. I think you are starting to see why this quickly became more complicated and expensive than I thought.

Basically, I would have to spend $80,000 cash (as I'm pretty sure they wouldn't take pelts in trade) just to secure financing for my property. I had paid a little bit of attention during my math classes, so I came to the quick decision that this was a bad idea.

I quickly realized that paying cash was the only realistic way to go. This meant the project would have to be done in phases, per my cash flow. The big advantage of this method, should you choose it, is that when your project is done you are debt-free. The down-side is that (unless you are independently wealthy) it could take forever to complete your home. This was something I faced because I come from a long line of poor people and there is no bank of "Gary's Family" from which I could withdraw or borrow.

So, to accelerate my project, I decided to look into a personal loan. However, I soon realized the interest rates were ridiculously high. They were just as high as or higher than my credit card interest rates. Well, that started to get the hamster running on the wheel in my head, and I realized I'm always getting "zero percent for 12 months" convenience check offers from my credit card companies. As I said earlier, I'm a big debt free guy, but I also realize sometimes you have to finance things short-term to get the project done before you are eating oatmeal for dinner and pooping in your diaper.

However, sometimes you have to think big picture and make some compromises to get the job done now instead of later. So I decided I would cap the money I borrowed to a number that was manageable for me. This way my debt would be controllable and I could pay it back in less than a year.

After talking with my local bank, I found another great nugget of information: Just because you can't finance the property by traditional methods, doesn't mean you can't get an equity line of credit once your house is built. In addition, you can wrap other short-term debt (credit cards, car loans) into your home equity line if you want.

Now, do you remember how, throughout this book, I have recommended always building to code, pulling the proper permits, and just generally doing everything according to local laws? Here's where this really comes back into play. To get a home equity line of credit, you will need something called an owner occupancy certificate. The only way you can get this certificate is by owning a home that passes all inspections and meets the building codes of your county upon completion. Completion can mean 95 percent done, or close to completion. This nuance is up to the discretion of the county inspector's office and the bank. Ultimately, to get the home equity line of credit, you will need to satisfy both your county inspector's and your bank's requirements.

Are you starting to see why it's important to build to code instead of trying to buck the system and cut corners?

After doing all this myself, I found out that this is the method most people use to complete their off-the-grid houses. First, they leverage short-term debt to get the project done. Then, they wrap the debt in a home equity line of credit that can be spread over 10-20 years. So, while I thought I had created this strategy all on my own, I later discovered that it had been done before.

Obviously, I do not recommend going into debt beyond your means, nor is this a blanket endorsement of the above method. In my situation, I found this to be effective, but it doesn't necessarily mean it will be right for you. Remember also that I made sure I could pay my debt back within a reasonable time frame. By the time my project was done, I was already debt-free, *and* I owned my house outright. I can't tell you how liberating this felt, but believe me that it's pretty, pretty, pretty darn good!

Off-The-Grid Home Construction

THE MOST COMMON TYPES

here is no cookie-cutter method when it comes to building an off-the-grid home. It is a novel and subjective experience for everyone. Deciding which size, materials, and type of construction to use for your home will depend on many factors that are specific to you.

As I have said in many chapters in this book, this section is not intended to be an all-inclusive, highly detailed manifesto on all "green" or off-the-grid homebuilding options. There are so many choices when it comes to construction, there is no way I could cover it all. Instead, I will cover the most common home types that are used for off-grid houses. These were the designs I researched and believe to be the most practical for the majority of people who want to live this type of lifestyle.

Since I started my project, I have met several people who have built off-grid houses, and the common theme has been that—construction-wise—every project is very different. I have yet to meet one person who has done it the exact same way as someone else.

The key factor in almost all off-grid home construction (unless you can afford a large alternative energy system, those people tend to use more traditional construction) is energy efficiency. Unless you have unlimited resources to invest in a giant alternative energy solution, this should always be the biggest factor guiding your construction decisions. Off-the-grid houses must retain their heat when it is cold, and stay cool when it is hot. This can be tricky since most off-the-grid homes lack a centralized, forced-air heating and cooling system. Indeed, these types of creature comforts—as well as other energy-guzzling appliances—just take too much energy to operate.

With off-the-grid construction, most houses and structures are built with "green" or recycled materials. These are materials that are considered more environmentally friendly, and in most cases have better insulation values, thus conserving more energy.

Building materials typically considered to be 'green' include lumber from forests that have been certified to a third-party forest standard; rapidly renewable plant materials like bamboo; and recycled stone, recycled metal, and other products that are non-toxic, reusable, renewable, and/or recyclable.

Simply put, green building practices aim to reduce the environmental impact of the building process. There are many different ways to do this, and again, it is highly subjective. With that being said, be careful, as many contractors have caught on to this trend. Many will call themselves "green builders", when they are anything but. Instead of being truly environmentally conscious, they are just looking to relieve you of some of that green material in your wallet.

Construction Methods

Type 1: Standard or "Stick" Construction

Standard or stick construction is what I consider to be the cheapest, and I believe, the easiest type of construction. This is the construction method used to build the majority of the houses in the United States today, primarily because it is cheap, quick, and takes the least amount of skill (my opinion). Standard construction usually consists of a concrete slab/foundation, but can have a raised crawl space, framed with standard 2x4, 2x6, or 2x8 pieces of wood, depending on your insulation and construction strength needs, and local building codes. This is the type of construction you will see in almost every neighborhood in the United States. A perfect example of this type of home is your standard tract house. In case you're not familiar with the term, tract housing is the style of building you see in suburban neighborhoods where rows of similar looking homes are built on their individual, standard sized lots.

PROS: The advantage of stick (or tract) construction is that the materials are easy to find and are "off the shelf". That is, you don't have to order them from a specialty manufacturer. It also tends to be a cheaper type of construction. Although it's almost exclusively used by general contractors, it can be a do-it-yourself (DIY) project and usually requires no specialty tools.

CONS: The disadvantages are that this type of build is usually not energy efficient, is typically not fireproof (this is a big deal in densely wooded areas), and is not as structurally stable as other types of construction in high wind areas.

Type 2: Straw Bale Construction

Straw bale construction is becoming increasingly popular for people living off-the-grid. These types of houses are usually built in low humidity areas due to possible moisture and rot issues.

Straw bale construction employs bales of straw as a structural and insulation material. The straw—which is simply dried stalks of grain—can be from a variety of crops, such as wheat, rice, rye, or oats. Bales can also be made from other fibrous materials, such as bean or corn stalks, pine needles, or any kind of grass.

The easiest way to describe straw bale construction is to think of hay bales stacked on top of each other with construction framing for structural support. The whole thing is then sealed with a stucco type of material. So, if you use straw bale construction, you will still have to frame your house, usually in a manner that is similar to the standard stick construction mentioned above (using traditional framing is usually the only way to meet structural code requirements with a straw bale approach).

PROS: The primary advantage of this approach is that straw bale homes have very high insulation values, thus making them very energy efficient. Another supposed advantage is that it can be an inexpensive type of construction, although I have not found this to be true. From my research and talking to people who have gone this route, it is far more expensive than what many building magazine and blog articles would have you think. I believe this is because the straw bale method is considered a specialized type of construction (therefore requiring specialized labor and/or materials that are not readily available) and presents the challenges of trying to get this type of structure to meet local building codes (again, extra time and money).

CONS: The disadvantages of straw bale construction are an increased susceptibility to rot due to moisture and the difficulty of obtaining insurance coverage. You can also look forward to infiltration by pests and rodents, and large space requirements for the straw itself (walls can be two to three feet thick).

Type 3: Log Construction

Log construction has been popular for a very long time, especially in wooded or mountainous regions. Such areas are usually remote and difficult to reach, so using the surrounding trees as your primary building materials is an easy and practical way to go.

Log construction is simply the practice of stacking notched tree logs in an interlocking pattern. This is how a standard log cabin is built. Log cabins today range from basic to very complicated and ornate.

I know a lot of popular "simple living" type of TV shows have made the log cabin look incredibly simple and cheap to construct, but this is usually not the case. I do know people who have built a log cabin without any outside help, but that is not the norm.

Conversely, log cabins are usually very expensive to construct when using a general contractor and can be flat out dangerous for the inexperienced "do-it-yourselfer". Think about cutting, moving, and stacking logs that weigh several hundred pounds each. Sounds like a perfect combination of dangerous activities by which you can get yourself seriously injured or killed.

Don't get me wrong, pioneers did this type of construction all the time, but they were a little tougher and more skilled in this area than us modern softies. If you are going to try it anyway, always keep your cell phone handy or have a friend work alongside you. The last thing you want is to be injured during construction, alone in a remote area, and without any way of calling for help.

PROS: The advantages of traditional log cabins are that they are built from green renewable materials, they are energy efficient and durable, it usually doesn't take much time to construct a cabin, and they look fantastic.

CONS: The disadvantages are that they can be expensive to build, must be constantly maintained (since wood dries and settles). They also need constant exterior care, can be fire hazards, and since pests and animals love wood, your home might become their dinner table and home as well.

Originally, I really wanted to build a log home, but it was just too expensive and would require too much future maintenance for me to even think about. I did contemplate going full blown DIY and using the trees on my property, but I just didn't have the knowledge or skills to go that route.

Finally, one of the main goals for my structure was for it to be virtually fireproof. So a log cabin was definitely not the right option in the end. But I still love log cabins, and it is on the list to have before I die. I just don't want to die building it.

Type 4: Cinder Block/ Insulated Green Block Construction

In this section, I will discuss both standard cinder block construction and green brick construction, since they have a lot of similarities. The only real differences are what the blocks are made of and the insulation value of each.

Cinder blocks are made from a combination of Portland cement and cinders (the dusty remnants of burned coal). In contrast, green brick products are usually made from recycled wood chips and concrete. Green blocks made from recycled wood have a higher insulation value than standard cinder block. In the industry these "green blocks" are called "Insulated Concrete Forms" (ICF).

Another form of ICF construction that has become very popular is Styrofoam walls filled with concrete. However, in some cases these are not considered green construction. They do have an incredibly high insulation value. The downside is they take a lot of concrete. So you will need good roads and access to get a concrete truck to your property.

Block construction is very basic and many industrial and commercial buildings use this type of construction. It simply involves stacking concrete or green blocks into walls and filling open cells with concrete and rebar for strength.

The advantages are: a low cost, lower insurance premiums, durability, pest/animal resistance, ease of construction, lower maintenance, good insulation value, outside-to-inside noise reduction, plus, they are fireproof.

The disadvantages are that they can be ugly if left unfinished, and it's more difficult to route electrical wires, plumbing, and other cabling within the house.

For me, after weighing cost, ease of building, location, and the need for a high insulation value, I decided to go with a recycled block product called *Faswall*. I don't intend to endorse one type of construction over another. There are a lot of factors you will have to consider when picking the type of construction and materials that are right for you. There are many other types of construction that fit into the off-the-grid lifestyle, but these three are the most commonly used, and therefore the easiest to research.

Some of you may even decide to combine different methods of construction. Heck, you might even invent your own. Just remember the farther you get from some of the more common construction methods, the harder it gets to comply with modern building codes, this will almost certainly mean higher building costs, and you may not be able to insure your dwelling because of this.

Getting Your Hands Dirty— Finding The Right Tools for Your Job

Unless you have unlimited resources, plenty of time, and the patience to have others do your work for you, you will probably have to learn a lot of new skills as you construct your off-grid home.

When constructing and living in an off-the-grid building, it is essential to have a good set of tools. Growing up in the sticks, I have had at least a basic set of tools since I was probably around 10 years old. After all, my Evel Knievel style bike jump ramp was not going to build and fix itself. (For you youngsters: Evel Knievel was a famous motorcycle stuntman.) So very early on I was using my hands, my own tools, and my Dad's tools to fix and build things (without his permission . . . most of the time).

Once I got older and purchased my first property, these tools and skills became incredibly handy. As any homeowner knows, things constantly need fixing! I still had a lot to learn, but knowing some basic fix-it principles was a huge help.

After realizing that contractors are expensive and (usually) a pain in the butt to deal with, I started doing most of the work on my homes myself. I actually did almost all the remodeling work on my first place by myself. Truth be told I didn't have a clue what I was doing, but I purchased numerous books on home renovation and just figured it out. Today, YouTube has a video on pretty much every type of remodeling or building project. This makes it far easier to learn these skills and see how they are performed.

A word of warning: Any idiot can make a video and post it on YouTube. I saw a show recently showing a young couple who decided to build and live remotely exclusively using YouTube videos for their information. I haven't seen an update to see if they have been eaten by a bear or starved to death, but it looked like they were well on their way to that.

Now, I know some of you more experienced folks may take the list below as common sense. Here is the deal—today most people have seen a hammer (on the internet more than likely), but have never swung one, and have no clue what it is for, except possibly to do great harm to their significant other after watching that real-life murder documentary. So you "old super-experienced curtsies" keep your derogatory comments to yourself and skip to the next chapter, because I'm doing this for the rookies.

Essential Hand Tools

Instead of giving you a long list of basic tools, I recommend you get a "homeowner's tool set/kit". These are basic sets that contain a multitude of tools commonly used for homeowner projects such as a hammer, screwdrivers, wrenches, a socket set, a tape measure, and so on. These usually run from $50 to $100 for a decent starter set. No, you can't build a house with these, maybe a doghouse, but these are just to get your feet wet without a large investment.

Don't buy these and run to your land in the woods thinking that is all you need to get familiar with basic tools before you even hammer that first nail on your property.

The reason I recommend this for beginners is that it's a cheap and easy way to get started. Tools can be very expensive, so until you get more familiar with them and figure out exactly what you need, the tool kit is a great way to get started. And last I checked no one has cut off their hand or killed themselves with this starter set.

As a matter of fact, I carry one of these "homeowner tool sets" in my travel trailer, so I don't have to carry a bunch of expensive individual tools that I will probably not use on a regular basis and will just take up space.

Once you graduate from your basic "cheap" tool set you can move on to big boy and girl tools you will need for your project.

Power Tools

Over the years, there is a basic set of power tools that I have used for a majority of my handy work. Here is the list I think everyone considering an off-grid journey should have:

DRILL/DRIVER: This is primarily used for drilling holes but can drive screws and small bolts.

IMPACT DRIVER: This is used primarily for driving (or removing) screws and bolts. Differs from drill/driver in that has more torque and has a fast-moving hammer that continually pounds the bit, letting you ease up on the pressure you would normally have to exert.

SAWZALL (RECIPROCATING SAW): This is considered the workhorse of demolition tools, as it is compact and can cut through wood and steel.

CIRCULAR SAW (SKILL SAW): This is a small handheld saw that can cut most wood construction materials. Different blades allow you to cut through concrete and steel as well.

MITER SAW: This is more of a specialty tool but one I have used a lot over the years. This will make quick work of miter cuts (angled cuts), such as those used on baseboards, crown molding, and cabinet finishing work.

CUT-OFF GRINDER: For me, this is probably one of the most versatile tools I own. For a metal fabricator, this is a must-have tool, but it can also be used to make difficult cuts with different blades on wood, concrete, and tile. I have primarily used this for cutting steel or metal piping and for tough angled tile cuts.

With the advancement of cordless tools, we off-the-grid enthusiasts now have a great set of resources to perform jobs that, in the past, used to require a generator and a spaghetti bowl of extension cords. You can get a decent set of the above listed tools, cordless, for about $500 to $600. (Note that you will still have to plug in the battery chargers for cordless tools somewhere, but they become ultra-portable throughout your work site without the need for wires!)

The contractor (professional) grade of these cordless power tools costs more because they usually have more torque and a longer battery life.

Now if you have never used power tools before, I wouldn't recommend you buy a set and just go for it. There are many professionals in the construction business missing fingers because of accidents. Power tools are very dangerous and can injure or even kill you or someone else if used improperly.

If there is a large hardware store (such as Home Depot) in your area, consider attending one of the numerous how-to classes they offer on home improvement and tool usage. These classes are typically free, so the price is right! The last thing I want to see is someone who read my book missing a finger, a hand, or a head. So always educate yourself first on how to use tools with which you are unfamiliar.

This is a fact: I know several people personally who were unfamiliar with using power tools that are now missing body parts, and/or physically disfigured. Just in case you were wondering . . . I still have all my limbs, toes and fingers. It would be rather difficult to be a writer with some missing fingers or a missing hand!

One more safety tip: "I can't emphasize this enough" always, always wear eye protection when using power tools. As a matter of fact, I would recommend safety glasses when using any type of tool. I have lost count how many times a piece of debris has been deflected away from my eyes and I was spared injury because I wear eyeglasses. During jobs where debris is flying all over the place I wear vented goggles that go over my glasses. They are cheap and readily available at any hardware store, and a couple bucks is worth it unless you like the nickname "one eye".

Also consider industrial noise-blocking ear protection, especially if you frequently use power tools (there are a lot of long-time builders out there with hearing problems!), and a hard hat if there will be overhead hazards at your work site. Again, all are inexpensive and easy to find at the hardware store.

Yard Tools

This is a pretty basic list of yard tools to get you started. Depending on your project, and the type of yard you plan to have and maintain, this list may quickly expand. However, I have found these five yard tools are the ones I use the most.

DIGGING SHOVEL: Talk about one of the oldest, but most-used tools around today. Dig holes, move dirt, move rocks, mix concrete, chop tree roots, take care of that annoying significant other . . . the many uses just keep on going.

POST-HOLE DIGGER: (manual, not powered): If you live off-the-grid or in the sticks, you will be digging fence postholes. It is a cheap and back-saving tool that I highly recommend.

HAND AX: Most off-gridders will have trees on their property, so a small ax is a great tool for cutting down small dead trees and removing limbs without having to use a chainsaw.

STEEL RAKE: This is not to be confused with a leaf rake that is for those yuppies in the suburbs. This is the tougher version with teeth spaced farther apart and made of hardened steel. You will be raking up many types of heavy debris and smoothing dirt on a remote property, so this is a must.

WHEELBARROW: Besides moving dirt, debris, materials, and tools around, it is a great tool in which to mix concrete by hand.

Obviously, there are many more tools that can and will be used on your off-the-grid property. But over the years I have found the above tools to be the most commonly used in everyday projects. Depending on your preference of buying used or new, the price of the tools will vary. Even if you decide to purchase all these recommended tools brand new, they can all be had for well under $1,000 if you take your time when shopping and get them on sale.

That is not bad when you consider that—with some creativity—you could build an entire house with just these recommended tools. Tools also hold their value well, so you can easily resell them if you exit the off-grid life.

Conversely, if you don't buy these tools, you are going to have to pay someone who does own tools to come and do every handyman and yard project that pops up. Over the long run, that will be much, much more expensive.

Off-The-Grid Security

IGNORE IT AND SOMEONE WILL GLADLY TAKE YOUR STUFF!

W e often assume that living remotely and off-the-grid means we're removed from the problems of living in urban society. I'm talking about having our houses broken into or our property stolen or vandalized. In many ways, living off-the-grid complicates these problems, which I'll explain in this chapter. The bottom line is criminals live in both rural and urban areas. Nevertheless, off-gridders often ignore or greatly underestimate the importance of off-grid property security.

So, in this chapter, I will describe how I also underestimated the immediate need for an effective security system for my own property and how you can avoid my mistakes.

When living remotely, some people assume that they will be able to completely disappear and that no one will bother them. From my experience this is not true at all.

Sure, if you really want to live like a hermit, you might be able to mostly remove yourself from human contact. However, I would say this is a rare exception rather than a common rule. In most instances, no matter how you decide to start your off-the-grid lifestyle, you will be surrounded by other people and you will have neighbors. Sure, they may be farther away, but they will be there even if you can't see them.

On top of this, people living remotely are much more in tune to new people moving into their area—especially compared to people living in a more urban area. The populations in rural areas are typically less transient and more self-reliant than in the city. So someone buying property in the area can be a newsworthy story. And they will more than likely be checking out what you are up to without you knowing it.

In fact, before you sign the final purchase agreement on your property, people will be talking about you. You'll be the new kid in the neighborhood. Remember that in small communities, information travels quickly and usually everyone knows everyone. So trust me: They will know you are coming and what your plans are, before you unpack your first box.

Now this is not to scare you away from off-the-grid living, but to enlighten you about what it means to have neighbors in remote areas. No matter how far away you are or how remotely you build your house, they are going to know about you. Humans are curious creatures and they love to talk, and that doesn't change when you're living off-the-grid. Now, let's talk about why this is essential to the safety of you and your personal property.

Lessons Learned— Why Security Should Be a Priority

When I began my off-grid lifestyle, I had a plan for my perimeter and basic security. However, I did not make it a priority because I didn't fully grasp the idea that I just laid out above. In my naïveté, I thought no one would really know or care what I was up to until I got further along in the construction and development of my property. Not only was I wrong, but I was wrong big time.

The first clue was when a neighbor in the area sat just off my property line and watched the initial construction of my road for an hour or so. I took this as just basic curiosity, which it could have been. However, shortly after that the following incident made me put my security plan into motion, and much more quickly than I had intended.

Not too long after getting the roadwork completed, it was time to get my well drilled. I didn't realize this at the time, but eyes were on me and on what I was doing. Remember, the drilling rig couldn't get to the top of my property and had to be towed by a bulldozer. We barely got it in place before dark. This was on a Friday, meaning that the drilling rig would be up at the property over the weekend with no one up there to watch over it (my house wasn't constructed yet). I also had no fences, gates, or security cameras at this time.

My attitude was that there was nothing of real value on my property. So, I thought leaving the drilling rig up there wouldn't be a big deal. That was another mistake. I live in a much wooded area known for logging . . . heck, my property was a former logging site, and tree poaching is a huge problem in the area . . . still is!

Again, I had initially thought about putting up a security system for the property. But I had another concern: I didn't know if I was going to have a water source until the well was drilled. So setting up a security perimeter and/or system was a financial risk, because if we couldn't find water I would have to re-evaluate my plans for the property.

So, I left my property unattended on a dark Friday night, with a $200k dollar drilling rig sitting right out there in the wide open. Call it spider-senses or just dumb luck, but something made me head up to the property the next morning. As soon as I got up to the spot where the drilling rig was parked, I noticed something seemed out of place. I did a quick walk around the rig and noticed one of its hoses on the ground and drag marks leading away up the hill to the other access road at the top of my property.

Upon further investigation, I noticed some small truck tire tracks and shoe prints. They were from more than one person. I immediately called the drilling company to let them know their drilling rig seemed to have been messed with, but I was unsure if anything had been taken.

When the drillers showed up Monday morning, they did an equipment check and found that their tire chains and hold-down straps had been stolen. These items were unsecured on the outside of the rig and worth about $200 a piece and weighed a total of about 350 pounds between them. Thankfully, no windows were broken, no attempt was made to break into the drilling rig, and no other vandalism had been done. As you can imagine though, I was more than upset that someone had stepped foot on *my property* and stolen something before I had even started any real work. Keep in mind that my nearest neighbor is probably a mile away. So, this little thieving operation would have required some planning, especially considering that the window of opportunity was only one night.

Tire chains are about 50 pounds each and all four of them were gone. Now nobody is going to walk at least three miles round trip onto private wooded property with about 200 pounds of chains. Remember this is not "the city night", with lights everywhere from buildings, street lamps and your neighbors that can hear you playing music. We are talking *"Blair Witch Project"* pitch-black forest night, so walking three miles is out. They drove onto my property for at least a mile and a half to reach the drilling rig, with the cover of night helping them out.

Initially, you might say this was a really bad start to my project. But you'd be underestimating how common this type of thing is while living off-the-grid. Looking back, I consider myself lucky to have gotten off with a couple of missing tire chains. This opened up my eyes to the fact that, just like any place in this country, people are looking to get something for nothing, or to create problems for you. Because this happened early on, I put my security plan into hyper-drive, and that simple fact probably saved me a lot of grief. If I had continued to put my security plan off, someone could have definitely stolen more expensive items later on, like my power tools, building supplies, guns, solar equipment, or even my truck.

Now I wasn't totally naïve. My original plan was to build my solar/storage shed as soon as we found water. This would be the place to store tools, and other items of value, so they would just not be out in the open. But I quickly learned my lesson—one that I hope you benefit from as well.

Instead of focusing exclusively on my power shed, I realized I needed to button up the access roads to deter people from entering my property. That would make it impossible for them to drive a vehicle right onto my property, load it up with ole' Gary's hard won possessions, and drive off without a hassle. It is a lot harder to haul items off by foot than it is to drive right up and load a vehicle or ATV and then drive away.

In my experience with law enforcement, I learned that thieves are usually not the most motivated individuals. Simply, the harder you make the job for them, the less likely they are to target your property.

Also, keep in mind that in rural areas, especially if your property has not been lived on for a while, well-intentioned locals may use it for hunting, hiking, or ATV rides. The good news is that this kind of person will eventually stop if you put up some basic gates and signage indicating the property is now private and in use. Of course, there are also thieves who need more clear indications your land is not easy to trespass upon.

Now, my first priority was making it hard for thieves to access my property. This meant placing gates (I chose re-enforced chain-link gates) in specific locations across my access roads. Here is where the hard-won lessons from my previous career dealing with security elements overseas came into play. Yes, criminals all over the world rely on similar tactics and are therefore deterred by similar security obstacles.

My advice is to make your property harder to access and thus discourage would-be thieves, you need two security access points for each road. In other words, someone should have to get through two security points instead of one, like the standard "Keep Out" gate most people would use. Does this mean more costs for gates and fences and the like? Yes, but trust me it is well worth it!

Gary's Security System and Recommendations

Obviously, I'm not going to reveal all the components of my security system and make this book a manual for stealing Gary's stuff. You know, like those people who post on Facebook when they are going on vacation. Thieves love stupid people, so it's good advice not to be one by advertising all your secrets or publicly announcing your comings and goings. However, I will give you the nuts and bolts of what has worked for me so that you can also implement a well-thought-out security system for your property. Of course, you will have to alter my plan as needed once you determine what your security needs and financial capabilities are.

First, you need to decide where to put your initial gate or road-access blocking point. Start by figuring out where it will be most difficult for someone to circumvent your gate (drive around it) with a vehicle or ATV. You have to realize there is no way to prevent people from walking onto your property. That is, unless you plan to set up miles and miles of Constantine wire, electrified fencing, land mines etc. Not to mention that if they are motivated, they can get around these traps anyway.

Basically, there is no perfect security system. So your goal is to make access more difficult and to discourage people from targeting your property instead of settling for the "low hanging fruit" of a neighbor who has less vigorous security than you. Putting in fences and gates isn't cheap, and on large properties, it is unrealistic to fence your entire perimeter. In most cases, you must select the best locations for your gates and fencing. To get the most bang for your buck, start by putting gates in strategic places.

One of the biggest mistakes I have seen over the years is the average homeowner's tendency to just throw up any inexpensive gate they can find. Don't do it! You have to look at your gate as the entryway to your way of life. This is an incredibly important part of your security system. When someone sees a well thought-out and robustly manufactured gate, they know you mean business, and it sends a stronger message.

I've lost count how many cheap gates I have seen smashed into a pile on the side of someone's property entry road over the years. When I see this, I have a pretty good idea of what happened, and it probably isn't good. But imagine being a thief and seeing a heavily fortified gate with clear warning signs about not trespassing. This could conjure up images of a thick-bearded property owner armed with military-grade firearms and his own pack of well-trained man-eating attack dogs. That's enough to make you rethink your gate breaking plans.

The pole to which your gate is mounted and attached needs to be as strong as possible, as this will be the primary failure point if done on the cheap. I used eight-foot tall, four-inch thick galvanized poles for some of my more strategic gates. Each one weighs around 100 pounds so these are seriously strong poles. These are the same size poles you will usually see on corner security fences that house things like heavy equipment, or storage units.

In addition to these gates, I dug, and in some cases air hammered, two to three foot-deep holes and filled them with two to three 80-pound bags of concrete to make sure these were absolutely as strong as possible. In addition, I filled the inside of each of the four-inch poles to within six inches of the top with concrete. You can now see that each pole consists of about 500 pounds of steel and concrete.

You are probably asking why would I go to the effort of filling the poles with concrete? For two reasons. First, if someone (including yourself) runs into it with a vehicle, it will not dent or bend the pole, therefore ruining your hard work. A bent gate pole is pretty much useless and replacing one that weighs 100 pounds is not fun. Secondly, if some genius decides they are just going to cut your pole down, they'll get a nice surprise when they hit the concrete at the center.

I'm not going to candy coat it: Putting in poles this size is a lot of work. But once in, they are rock solid and are not going anywhere. Sure, you can use wood to save money, I have in certain spots, but a determined thief can make quick work of them with just a hand saw. Now if you want to save money, and your gate is within view of a neighbor, a big wood pole works just fine.

Now that you have put all this time and effort into your gate poles, don't just throw up any gate. Make sure it is strong and reinforced. My "don't think about it" gates and fencing are all chain-link. Considering the money and the ease of setting it up, I have found chain-link fencing a great choice. Chain-link fencing now comes in different colors. So if you don't like the look of it, you can now get it in a color that lets it fade into the landscape.

The other thing I like about chain-link fencing is the ease with which you can install barbed wire on top. There is no better deterrent than three-string flesh-gouging barbed wire at the top of your fence. I have barbed wire on some of my fencing and gates. Again, ol' Johnny Dirt Bag thief doesn't want to get all cut up, so this will definitely make him think twice about jumping over your fence.

One last little trick to help secure your fencing is to either spot weld or to apply JB Weld (an epoxy that bonds to metal) to all the fastening nuts and bolts. You have to love thieves; some spend a lot of time and energy trying to figure out how to steal your stuff. By welding or putting JB Weld on all your fence fasteners, you make sure they will not be able to unscrew your fence attachment points and just walk or even drive right in. Getting easy access to your property usually means unscrewing only three or four bolts on the connection pole of your fence. This simple trick will stop them.

As I have said, there is no perfect system to keep people out. You just want to make it as hard on them as possible. The more time they have to spend trying to get onto your property, the more likely it is that someone will see or hear them. Not to mention the fact that you will get some nice video or photos of them on your security cameras while they're hard at work trying to get through your security gates. Speaking of security footage . . .

Off-The-Grid Security Cameras

I've spent many, many hours researching video camera systems, and let me tell you, there are tons. They can range from very simple cameras that cost less than a hundred dollars, to complex systems costing thousands. The technology is changing so quickly that I will not dedicate very much time to this subject, as it will be outdated by the time this book is released. Your choice of security camera will also be highly specific to your needs and your type of property.

I will say this: When it comes to home security camera systems, the sky is the limit. There is a camera solution for almost any situation. Systems are now even completely wireless and can be quickly installed by the non-professional. In addition, most can send data straight to your computer and cell phone in real time, which is especially helpful when you are not at your property year-round.

The biggest factor, when it comes to security camera systems of today, (and this could change) is they must have a continuous internet connection through a router in order to work (more on this later).

Here is my recommendation for off-gridders wanting to have a simple, yet effective, off-grid security camera system. A game camera (also known as a trail camera) is a remote camera designed for hunters. It is weatherproof and built for extended, unmanned use outdoors. It can be mounted to a tree and is used to record video or still images. Game cameras are motion-sensitive; meaning that the recording or photo is usually triggered by the movement of animals (bipedal hairless ape trespassers in this case). Hunters use game cameras to surveil and scout game, but they make great off-grid security cameras as well.

Most game cameras only record videos and/or take photos that are stored on a SIM Card (data storage card). If you want to see the pictures, you have to get to the camera itself and remove the card. In contrast, I like and use game cameras that have the ability to communicate via cell phone towers, thus sending data directly to your computer and/or cell phone. I prefer this to internet-based cameras (such as webcams) because internet connections can drop out and are susceptible to power outages.

The great thing about the game cameras with cellular communications is that you can put them anywhere there is cell phone coverage. Today this means a fairly wide spread of being able to use these types of cameras. Game cameras can also run on an external power supply (even small solar panels) or on batteries. They are also designed to be unobtrusive and to blend into a natural background, making them hard for criminals to spot.

Not only will you get some great photos of the local wildlife but also of any person who trespasses and wanders into the camera's view. This way, if someone breaks into your outbuilding, vehicle, or home, you will hopefully have a nice picture or video of the culprit to show to the police.

So, game cameras are an excellent security solution for off-grid living. They are also durable. One of my cameras is still up and running with full battery reading after two years of use. I use long-life lithium batteries, which I do recommend, as they last much longer than your standard batteries.

Game cameras are a great supplement to, or backup for, a standard video camera system. The cameras I use are the *Bushnell* wireless version. They have changed over the years—I have some that are older and a couple that are newer. I would love to give you the names and models, but it appears they have changed more than once. Simply, go to www.bushnell.com, check the wireless box in the game camera section and they should come up.

High Tech Off-The-Grid Security with Camera Triangulation

Cameras are pretty expensive, which means Johnny Dirt Bag loves stealing them. I have lost count of people who have told me they have had their game cameras stolen. Thankfully, there are several ways to make sure your security cameras don't end up for sale in local pawnshops (a favorite place for thieves and meth heads to sell your goods).

The first way to protect your cameras is a basic security method I call camera triangulation. This means that all your security cameras are pointed at each other from three separate points, creating a triangle. Meaning, camera number one points at camera number two, camera number two points at camera number three, and camera number three points back at camera number one.

This way, the space you want to monitor goes in the middle of this triangle. By pointing each camera at the other in this type of triangular arrangement, you guarantee that if someone tries to steal one of your cameras, another camera will record the theft. Make sure the cameras are not easily seen, and you will get some great shots of the thief as he thinks he's stealing your only camera, but your other camera is recording his deed. The great part is that if you're using the wireless setup, you'll have these videos on your phone even if he does take all your cameras. If this happens with traditional game cameras, no such luck.

If you want to be really devious, set up a bait or dummy camera (just a shell; not a functioning camera). Set up the bait in the open so that the thief cannot miss it. This will do one of two things: It will scare off the thief, because he realizes your "private property" signs mean business and you actually do have cameras. Or, the stupid thief will look at it as an item to steal. So, while Johnny Dirt Bag is attempting to take your camera, a hidden, real, functioning camera will record him stealing a worthless piece of plastic.

Most thieves aren't the brightest lights in the bunch, so putting a little thought into your security is worth the time and effort. By doing it right, you will greatly decrease your odds of becoming a victim. Better yet, even if you are, you will have a ton of evidence to give to law enforcement. Trust me, in small towns people talk. If someone gets arrested because of a crime that you recorded on camera using your slick security system, everyone will know you are not to be messed with. Matter of fact I get some funny comments from people who do not know me, but know of my property, such as "you are the guy with the cameras all over the place" or "you are the one with the compound." I'm not offended one bit. These comments mean what I have done is working just like I want it to.

Some other security tips: You can purchase a game camera with a lockbox, which I highly recommend you do. In case you're unfamiliar, a lock box is a locked box that your camera sits in while it's working, so that anyone stealing it will have to break into the box to get at the camera. Sure, they can still take the entire setup, box and all, but they'd look awful suspicious trying to sell that to a pawn shop owner without the key or the lock combination. Make sure to purchase a lock box made of steel and not some other flimsy material. Depending on your location, you can also mount it quite high on a tree, so that any would-be camera thief would need a ladder or some serious climbing skills to reach it. All my cameras have lock boxes with a heavy-duty combination lock.

Dogs—Man's Best Friend
Can Be a Thief's Worst Deterrent

Over my years in law enforcement, the one thing my co-workers and I always dreaded having to deal with when serving search warrants was a dog. There were a few times I thought I was going to have to shoot a suspect's dog because it looked pretty vicious. Luckily, they all ended up being big wimps in the end. Being a dog lover, the last thing I wanted to do was shoot man's best friend. But I tell this story to emphasize what a deterrent a good sized, scary looking dog can be. The bottom line is that dogs are a great supplement to your security system.

As a matter of fact, as long as I have owned dogs, I have never had one of my properties broken into. Remember that thieves are opportunists, so the harder you make it for them to break in, the more likely it is that they will move on to a softer and easier target. Dogs bite and make noise, so most thieves want nothing to do with them. And if Johnny Dirt Bag is stupid enough to take a shot at or shoot your dog, he opens up an entire different can of worms because almost all off-gridders are armed . . . very bad move!

I would highly recommend a big dog for security purposes. Don't get me wrong, small dogs can be vicious. My mom's little dogs have taken a piece of me on more than one occasion, but they are not very intimidating. If push comes to shove, your little dog will get taken out pretty easily. A big dog, however, is a different story. I spent years around K-9 handlers and their dogs, and I will tell you that having those dogs let loose is something that I would only wish on a very bad person. Even a fat lazy dog is faster than most (in shape humans) and can bite with hundreds of pounds of force per square inch. So, Johnny Dirt Bag knows he isn't getting away, and that bite is going to leave a serious mark!

Anyone who has been bitten by a large dog knows that they are not to be toyed with. I still have a couple of scars from my youth, put there by dogs that didn't want me in their area. I grew up in the sticks, so more than once I accidentally (okay, maybe purpose-fully) wandered onto private property and got a nice surprise for my stupidity.

A protective dog doesn't have to be some well-known guard breed like a Doberman or German Shepherd either. For example, I once had a chocolate Labrador named Brownie who was a great guard dog (she is now in doggie heaven). Labs are not really known for their viciousness, and they are very loyal and loving dogs, but Brownie (yes I named her that) could bark like a doggie cannon. I don't know how many people would avoid even knocking on my door because old Brownie was going nuts. Funny thing, she wasn't barking because she wanted to tear them a new one. It was her way of saying . . .

"Hurry up, get over here and throw the ball to me."

Like people, dogs have different ways of expressing themselves, and many times, their bark is more of a friendly "hello", than a warning. Thankfully, the average thief doesn't know what that dog bark means. For most of them, it isn't worth rolling the dice. Plus, the house could have an owner who is a staunch believer in the Second Amendment (most off-gridders are) and who is now well aware that someone is close by.

The best part was that Brownie's buddy, my other dog, was a Rottweiler named "Cybil". And no, I didn't name her and feel sorry for the person who did. Probably someone like my first off-the-grid realtor. Anyway, even though Cybil was pretty scary looking, most people never even noticed her because Brownie had their full attention.

Ok, now for Gary's disclaimer: I'm not recommending you go and get a dog that is trained to tear someone's throat or rip an arm out of its socket on your command. Many people have been killed in dog attacks that had nothing to do with criminal activity. You also need to be prepared to take on the responsibilities of the particular breed you acquire—some larger and currently trendy dog breeds may make great security deterrents, but also have difficult temperaments, high exercise needs, are challenging to train, and can be a very poor choice for inexperienced dog owners. So I'm not saying you should buy a dog strictly for their security value. I'm just saying that dogs are a great deterrent for those who may not have the best intentions when coming to your property.

The Reality of Off-The-Grid Health Insurance

There is one question that comes up every single time I give a live presentation about living off-the-grid, "How do I find and obtain affordable health insurance while living this lifestyle?" This isn't just a question for living off-the-grid. It also applies to being self-employed (which is the topic of the final chapter).

It just so happens that people who live or are looking to live off-the-grid are either self-employed, or want to be self-employed. As far as I know, living off-the-grid doesn't put you in some special category when it comes to health insurance plans.

My answer to this question is always the same: The best health insurance plan is to make sure you are as healthy as you can possibly be. This is why everyone who wants to live The Simple Life should buy and read my book *The Simple Life Guide to Optimal Health*. Time and time again I get approached by people who are in terrible shape (statistically that is most of America today) and their first off-the-grid question is about health insurance or how to access medical facilities. I cannot make it any plainer than this—if you plan to remain overweight, to eat like crap and neglect regular exercise, living off-the-grid is not for you!

Yes, this lifestyle is highly rewarding, and I truly love it. However, it is also not easy. It requires a lot of self-reliance and, unless you have gobs of money, you are going to be doing a lot of manual labor . . . on a consistent basis! Your firewood is NOT going to chop itself. Your roads will need to be maintained. If you are going to homestead, someone has to milk your cows, plant your crops and slaughter your chickens. This life is not a reality TV show and it's not for tourists.

The amount of care I take to avoid getting severely injured is pretty astounding. I think through every project, because in some cases it could be the difference between life and death. Health insurance is not going to fix that.

Some of you may think this is a cop-out or that I'm avoiding the question of health insurance. The simple answer is, I can't give you a shortcut on this and be an honest author. Finding affordable healthcare today is such a complicated issue that is changing all the time. There is no way I could do an adequate job of telling you the correct options for you. Health insurance companies are constantly going out of business or stopping coverage in certain states or areas. By the time this book hits the shelves there is a good chance any specific information I included would be obsolete. So, here is the best and straight-forward advice I can give in this matter: If your health is going to be a continual issue, you need to seriously evaluate whether this lifestyle is even an option. If you still want to live this lifestyle in spite of having health issues, you need to either pay out of pocket for a health insurance plan (none of them are cheap) or find a job that offers a good health insurance plan and allows you to work remotely.

If you cannot afford the health insurance you want, you need to make your health your number-one priority. In fact, you need to do that whether you can afford the health insurance plan you want or not. Too many people treat health insurance like a substitute for being in good health, when it should be a means of insuring yourself against an unexpected medical emergency, like an accident. The best way to minimize your reliance on health insurance is to take control of your own health. It is your health after all. If you expect someone else to take care of it for you, you are completely missing the point of living The Simple Life.

I suggest you find a doctor in your area who is willing to take cash payments for their services. In most cases doctors will offer a huge discount for payment if you pay in cash at the time of the service. Most of a doctor's overhead comes from dealing with insurance companies and the associated billing.

Also, make sure you set aside a medical emergency fund of five to ten thousand dollars. Yes, this is a lot of money, it is worth it when you consider that this money could help you get that unexpected surgery from the doctor you want.

See if there is a teaching hospital in your area that offers discounts for the uninsured or indigent care. That is, health services for people who do not have health insurance and who are not eligible for other health care such as Medicaid, Medicare, or private health insurance. Bottom line, the smartest health insurance policy is a good combination of financial planning and staying healthy. I know that this is probably not the answer people were looking for, but again every one's situation is different. This is something you need to research and figure out before you move past the "looking into" stage of living off-the-grid. The harsh reality is that wanting to do something has nothing to do with whether you're ready to do it. With that being said, I think most can live this lifestyle with no problem. That is, if they're willing to make some sacrifices.

Everything worth doing takes a lot of work and, most likely, a lot of personal growth. That is just life. Having access to health insurance and medical care is just one piece of a much larger puzzle, and there are no shortcuts. So, if you're serious about this lifestyle, I encourage you to make the right preparations by simplifying your life in all areas, health, finances, and your career.

That said, if there's one thing that can keep you Gridlocked and block you from ever living this lifestyle, it's being chained to a location specific job. So, let's finish up our study with some sound advice on how to start your own off-the-grid business.

Off-The-Grid Jobs
HOW TO MAKE A LIVING WHILE FOLLOWING YOUR DREAM

One of the most frequent questions I get while talking about off-grid living is, "How do I make a living and what kinds of jobs would you recommend for this type of lifestyle?"

First, let's start with a little tough love—if you struggle to make ends meet right now, you need a reality check before you decide to embark on this journey. I'm going to tell you from first-hand experience, trying to fix your employment and financial woes while attempting this lifestyle is a surefire path to an epic failure.

Living off-the-grid is not the solution to all your life problems. The problems you take with you in this lifestyle will still be there, and most cases will become magnified. If you have little or no experience making a consistent living, in a field that is somewhat stable, becoming a remote entrepreneur is going to be very hard for you, maybe impossible.

The False Prophets, who I mentioned earlier in this book, will tell you it is as simple as just buying a property, building a house or starting a homestead. Sure! Just get some goats, rabbits, chickens and bam . . . you are living the sustainable life of a true off-gridder! Of course, these authors also give you several ideas for starting a remote business. There are hundreds of copycat books on Amazon that "teach" you how to do all this. I know this because most of these authors have never done it themselves, and have simply copied the ideas in my books or someone else's.

Since most authors are busy selling you dreams of unicorns that poop gold nuggets and healthy cupcakes, it's my job to tell it like it is. I've watched time and time again rookie off-gridders, aspiring entrepreneurs, and hopeful homesteaders fail, fail and fail some more trying to build this kind of lifestyle! Matter of fact, I do not know one person who has successfully done this despite having no prior knowledge in at least some of the basic skills. I'm sure there are some rare freak of nature exceptions.

But most people have at least a bit of a plan. Even then, once reality hits they go into panic mode, lose a lot of money, have a great deal of unnecessary stress, and suffer multiple failures before they eke out a living, either by making a measly remote income, or end up back at their day job. Geez, I'm a real buzzkill, aren't I? Hey, I don't say this to discourage you. I'm a realist and not here to sell you bullshit. I'm starting with the bad news *because* I want you to succeed.

So, What Does it Take to Start a Remote Business?

Unless you're already working remotely and making a good and steady income, you need a solid plan for making a living and you need to be executing it with success before you begin your off-the-grid project. As I told you earlier, I spent years getting everything together before I put my plan into action. First, I decluttered my life by selling my house and all my unnecessary items. I also became debt free and 100 percent mobile, with nothing weighing me down. But the most important thing I did was create a mobile business—one by which I could make a remote living in preparation for my off-grid lifestyle.

I didn't just leave my stable life in the government, start my own business, and boom off to the races. I came up with a business that I enjoyed and could use to make a living from anywhere. Here is the big dose of reality—I worked numerous jobs in-between until I could finally support myself with my new business. This took years and it took a lot of soul searching and hard work. Over the years, I have received more e-mails than I can count, asking me how I did it, and if I could help someone start their own business as I did. This is not only the lazy way to go about it, it's also the wrong way to go about it.

I can only give you basic advice on what I have done, and firsthand knowledge of what has worked for myself and other people. But if there's one thing you can be certain of when starting your business is that your challenges will be completely unique to everyone else who has started a similar business. Those books that promise to give you the shortcuts, most of them are written by people who are trying to make money teaching you how to make money. You'd be shocked at how many of those authors have day jobs too.

Again, this is your life, not mine, or anyone else's. I don't have any magic bullet to success. That is on you. I can give you the perfect career that has worked for thousands in the nomadic and off-grid lifestyle, but if you don't plan and execute it with persistence, you will fail. I have met a lot of slackers who thought living off-the-grid was a great way to continue being a slacker. It never works out that way. Like anything else worth having, this lifestyle is the fruit of hard work and persistence.

That said, the first thing you definitely need to do is set at least a year of living expenses aside (outside of your off-grid project) before you start your remote business. Keep this money in a separate account and do not commingle it with your other funds. If you do, you will be tempted to dip into it as soon as you have unexpected expenses.

Secondly, these funds should be supplemented by the income generated from your successful remote business. This is pretty straight-forward, as it is exactly what I preach in my *Simple Life Guide to Financial Freedom* book . . . you should always have a year of living expenses in reserve just in case things go bad.

Before we jump into my business and career recommendations, let me give you a list of the jobs the False Prophets advise as a means of achieving remote financial freedom. These are "careers" I highly recommend you avoid like poison. Most of the time, these jobs are touted as "costs no money for startup and work just four hours a week to make six or seven figures" . . . if they want to lay it on extra thick. The truth is most of these jobs take years to become proficient in and to make a living at.

Of course, if you are already doing one of these jobs successfully that is a different story. I'm including this list of remote jobs because they are, most often, the "sucker bait" for luring people in with promises of an "easy" career which requires little or no prior experience. Again, reality check, this is complete bullshit and just designed to sell you books and products on how to get into these remote jobs. Trying to make a living in something you have zero experience at, while trying to live off-the-grid, is like expecting to find pots of gold at the end of rainbows and to spend the rest of your life eating zero calorie cupcakes and riding unicorns.

The Fool's Gold of Working Remotely

'll start with my very favorite BS make-a-living-remotely fairy dust. I am putting these three together as they usually go hand in hand.

BLOGGING, PODCASTING, AND AFFILIATE MARKETING: You know who makes money from these businesses? The people selling you the books or courses on how to make money doing these things. The big "secret" is that they're not making any money with these businesses themselves. They're simply trying to make money by telling you that you can make money doing these things. Most of them are failing at that too. This is why I often say . . .

> "If all marketers were as brilliant as they say they are they would all be rich following their own marketing advice in a REAL business."

I have yet to meet an honest "how to make money from home" guru who is rich as a result of following their own marketing advice. Instead, a lot of them are selling you a pipe dream, which they have no experience in. Their "advice" is not based in reality. The truth is, in almost all cases, blogging and podcasting actually cost you money. In most cases, blogging and podcasting are part of a bigger business model that is pretty advanced and which takes hard work to duplicate. There are very few people who make money off blogging or podcasting alone. I should know since I have had a blog and a podcast for years. Yes, there was a time when you could make a living affiliate marketing. In case you're unfamiliar with the term "affiliate marketing", this is when you earn a commission promoting and selling products through web-links on your website. You do not physically sell the products or deliver them. You simply send web traffic to the person who sells the products, hoping that the visitor buys the product so you can get paid a commission. The days of making money this way are pretty much long gone, and I'm talking years ago! Sure, some people still brag about the money they made when they first started affiliate marketing, but they're telling you old war stories from the early 2000s.

I personally do not know of anyone who makes a living using solely affiliate marketing. Yes, I do know people who run successful six-figure plus businesses who use affiliate marketing. However, their businesses have been around for a long time and the affiliate marketing side is not their main source of revenue.

SOCIAL MEDIA MANAGER / MARKETING EXPERT: This is another pipe dream people try to sell you on, just so they can make money selling you their "how to become a social media manager" products. Simply do a search on the internet or LinkedIn and you'll see how many hits you get on someone calling themselves a "Social Media Manager". You will get thousands and thousands. Why so many? Well, because someone conned them into thinking this was easy street to easy money. You'll also find TONS of them sending you spammy sales pitches on LinkedIn. They're doing this because they can't find customers, and read some False Prophet's stupid "how to find high-paying clients on LinkedIn" e-book or online course.

Ha, good luck with that. Just because most Americans are addicted to social media, doesn't mean social media "experts" are in high demand. Most of them are just dreamers who read a book on how to do it, and who simply haven't realized that it takes real experience to make it in this competitive space. Managing social media accounts for businesses is a very different ballgame, than being a user. On average I will get 10-15 solicitations a week from people calling themselves "Social Media Managers" or "Social

Media Experts". When I look into their background and experience, they have a big fat zero in terms of real expertise!

Here is another key factor: Most of us small business owners and entrepreneurs cannot afford to outsource our social media management to someone for the fees these people are asking, or any fee for that matter. Those of us who can afford it have dozens of things we'd spend that money on before we'd dream of dumping it into these kinds of services. This means your biggest customer base cannot afford your services, making this a pretty bad business model.

BECOMING AN AUTHOR: This one is close to my heart, because, well, I'm an author. If you want to pick a new career to not make any money in . . . ever, this is it. I have been writing for a decade now, and I'm nowhere near where I want to be. That will probably never change since I have high standards. But I'm doing better than 99.99% of independent authors, and I'm still not rolling in dough. Even after a decade, I spend a great deal of time trying to get better and better. Attempting to be a "paid" author is not something done on a whim.

Here is a fact that should drive it home: Last time I checked there are somewhere around 7 million books in digital format on Amazon. According to Amazon, only somewhere in the neighborhood of 1,500 authors of these 7 million books make six-figures or more. And six-figure total doesn't represent the money you'll actually take home. It doesn't include the cost associated with your time, professional cover design, editing, advertising and numerous other costs associated with self-publishing a book. Trust me, you are not the first person who thinks they have a best-selling juggernaut of a book just waiting to be published.

I'm in the self-publishing circles, and it is one of the biggest "fake it until you make it" careers I have found. As a former investigator, I have looked into these authors' backgrounds and I have lost count how many self-published authors claim to be making a living at it, but are either breaking even or losing money at it. In fact, I ran into one guy who claimed to be making over a hundred thousand a year. I later found out that this six-figure income came from his day job. When he lost that, he came to me looking for advice on how to make his writing business profitable. Regardless of what they tell you, it is pretty easy to see an author's ranking on Amazon and determine how much money they are making after they've paid their expenses.

On top of this, you'd be shocked at how many of those "I make six-figures writing books" people spend six figures in advertising to get to that six-figure income. Matter of fact I have met several New York Times "Best Selling Authors", who still have full-time jobs outside of being an author. I cannot emphasize enough how hard it is to make a living as an author. Only recently could I claim to be making a living as an author. However, I have other income sources, as should every smart author. You also have to remember that your earnings as an author are different every month. So, if you're looking for a steady income, this is definitely not something you should mess with.

On top of this all, even if you do become a self-published author who makes a full-time living, your income is not guaranteed in the future. In 2019, Amazon made a simple change to their search engine algorithm and caused a 50 percent drop in sales for thousands and thousands of authors. I know authors who went from making a full-time living to being forced back to work, and this happened almost overnight.

I will leave you with this—if you want to be an author you need to do it on the side while working on something stable that pays the bills. I know because this is what I did, and I know many others who followed this path to becoming an author.

BECOMING A SECRET SHOPPER: This will be short and sweet. If you think someone is going to pay you to buy products for a living, you're dreaming. This is a scam and has been since the days of the damn Yellow Pages! As a secret shopper, you have to buy the product with your own money. Then, you get reimbursed after you rate the store or give the product a review. Do you see anything fishy about this? Not to mention that if you are living off-the-grid, you probably won't be very close to a mall. I know there's not one on my property!

DATA ENTRY: First, let me say that I have nothing against data entry jobs. I have done them to pay the bills when I was younger, but I hated it. Living off-the-grid and enjoying The Simple Life isn't about doing something that will eventually drive you nuts! Not to mention that this is the bottom of the barrel when it comes to low paying jobs and will most likely be replaced by technological advancements over the next ten years. If you follow what I preach, which is living debt free, you might be able to get by on such a low-level job. But I wouldn't bank on it. Even if you could, there's no way you'll ever build any financial security, let alone wealth, when your income is this low.

VIRTUAL ASSISTANT: Okay, this is one that is doable. That is, if you have skills and experience in being a good assistant. A little personal story to share—I have had terrible luck hiring VAs. I have tried using them on several occasions for things that were taking my valuable time and needed to be offloaded. The result? I ended up wasting more time training and baby-sitting my VA. It would have been quicker to just do the work myself. Not to mention that being "ghosted" by a VA is a huge problem in the entrepreneurial world. The reason? Most of these "want to be" VAs have zero skills and/or just move on to the next "easy money from home" scam the second they realize that being a VA means actually doing work.

Now if you have the knowledge and experience as an assistant that is a bit of a different story. But you need to know that building up enough clients to pay the bills is not easy. There are tens and tens of thousands of people calling themselves VAs today and you'll be competing with them for clients. Again, this could be a decent side hustle, but I wouldn't treat it as your primary way to make a living.

I could go on and on, but I think you get the point. The above are the jobs most hopeful digital nomads or off-gridders get sucked into. And again, there are thousands of stupid books written by False Prophets, which promise you that the above jobs are the secret doorway into a virtual lifestyle. I'm not saying they are impossible to make a living at, I am saying that most of them are very difficult to make work. Another huge factor most wanna-be off-gridders ignore is that these jobs require consistent and speedy internet access.

Sure, the technology is getting better, but it is still not to the point where you can live an off-grid lifestyle and make these jobs a realistic possibility. Even to this day, I struggle getting consistent internet access to run my business, and I have been doing it for a long time.

Here are some of the others you should avoid (again unless you have years of experience and reliable internet access).

- Voiceover/Narrator
- Transcribing
- Travel expert
- Graphic design
- Programmer
- Taking online surveys
- Consultant in area you have NO expertise in (taking a course does not make you an expert)

Now let's live in the real-world and take a look at the jobs that make sense for living off-the-grid. Now I will warn you, unlike those "just sit in your underwear and make millions" jobs listed above, these require something called effort and hard work.

GET A REAL 9 TO 5 JOB: Oh, I know I just pissed a bunch of people off by not only putting this on the list, but putting it at the top. But hear me out before you throw this book into the fire or send me a profanity laced email. I discuss this in my other books and on my Your Better Life podcast in great detail. Being an entrepreneur and running your own business is not for everyone. And guess what? There is nothing wrong with that. I also want to make it clear that I know a lot of people who live off-grid who do not run their own businesses. Yes, this means you might not be able to live 50-100 miles out in the sticks. But that is not for everyone either. You can live a little off the beaten path, and off-the-grid while having access to a normal job. In fact, I live close enough to a big city and a couple small towns I could get a regular job if needed. Even though I run and own my own business, I also need to be somewhat close to an airport for travel. Again, this is your own adventure so you need to make something work for yourself, not me, or anyone else.

CONSTRUCTION: If you are able bodied, willing to learn new skills, and can work with your hands, this is by far the easiest job market to not only gain quick employment, but to earn a good living. If you doubt this, just remember that most of your "competitors" will be ole Mr. Joe Six-Pack. Now instead of going into a long list of all the professions in this area, let me give you a basic list:

GENERAL CONTRACTOR: This one takes experience and knowledge in the field.

LABORER: This is the grunt work of entry into the trades, but in many cases, you can also start working the day after being hired.

APPRENTICE: This is usually the next stage up after being a reliable laborer.

HANDYMAN: This is great if you are a jack of all trades, but not necessarily an expert. Even if you have little experience, you will be good enough for the person who wants a basic fence installed or a leaky faucet fixed. Especially if you know how to show up to work on time and actually return your client's calls.

I know a lot of off-gridders who do some form of the above-mentioned work. If you are willing to put in the time and learn some new skills, the following independent contracting jobs are almost always in huge demand:

- Welder/metal worker
- Mechanic
- Plumber
- Electrician
- Heavy machine operator

I've included this list for a few reasons. First almost anyone who knows how to work hard at learning a new (basic) skill can do them. It doesn't matter whether you're a woman or a man either. These professions are in demand almost everywhere. Heck, a lot of these have the potential to make you six figures. I know this first hand because, even in my small community, people are constantly looking for reliable professionals who have the above skills. Not to mention that I know numerous people in my area who have started their own business in the above trades and they have more work than they can keep up with.

There are also many types of businesses you can run out of your own property such as: knife making, ranching, farming, homeschooling/daycare, metal fabrication and bushcraft/survival skills training, just to name a few. As a general rule, avoid anything that promises you money without hard work, and find something you're confident that you can work hard at without getting bored or burning yourself out. You'll be surprised at how much financial opportunity there is if you stop chasing unicorns and start working hard at something that creates real value for people.

Of course, this isn't an A-Z chapter about how to make a living while going off-the-grid. There are just too many factors to consider, including your age, education, skills, work experience, location, your willingness to learn new things and your current financial status. All of these will determine what career choice will best serve you and your family.

We live in the most prosperous country in the world. Not only does everyone have the ability to live the life they want, they can also make a living doing something they truly enjoy. Again, simple living doesn't mean easy living. Work is work, there is no getting around that. Those who want to take short cuts and search for the next "make $50,000 a month while sitting in your bathrobe." are destined to waste time and money on products created by False Prophets. None of them will accomplish their dreams.

For most, finding the right off-grid career will take time, attention, and persistence. I know for a fact that my career has changed since I first started this adventure nearly a decade ago. But I kept at it, refining my process until I found something that worked for me. When I started out, I had no idea I'd end up doing what I am doing today. So, there is no way for me (or anyone else) to tell you exactly what to do, how to do it or whether you even should do it. I have received many emails over the years asking me for this kind of hand holding.

Believe me, if I had a perfect formula, I'd already be offering it as a book or training course. This is your career and you need to be proactive in finding it, I cannot and will not do it for you. Nor can anyone else. Anyone who tells you differently is trying to make a career out of selling pipe dreams to people who haven't learned this lesson yet.

Some Final Words:
Launching Your Own Off-Grid Dream

Years ago, I was stuck between paying an exorbitant mortgage on my massive house in one of America's most expensive zip codes, wrestling appalling traffic and pollution. All so I could get to my high-pressure job so I could pay for all the crap I'd collected over the years. For the sake of my own sanity and happiness, I decided there had to be a better way, a simpler way. If you've read this far, I'm guessing you have come to the same conclusion.

However, turning away from the convenience of public utilities and freeing yourself from the Cult of Clutter is an undertaking filled with many real-world challenges. It will require you to be self-reliant, innovative and (most likely), to learn a whole host of new habits and skills.

Nevertheless, returning to the true spirit of what America stands for—independence, personal freedom, and making your way in the world through your own efforts—can be one of the most rewarding journeys you will ever make. I've made a lot of mistakes in my life. But I've also made a number of strong strides along the way. Matter of fact, I hardly recognize the guy who started this journey all those years ago . . . and that's a good thing!

Through sharing all the lessons I've learned about selecting, powering, financing, building, and maintaining an off-grid home, I've also learned a lot about how I want to live my life. Henry David Thoreau said it all far more eloquently than I ever will in his 1854 memoir and spiritual dissertation, *Walden*. To write this American classic, Thoreau left traditional society to live alone, for two years, in a woodland cabin near Walden Pond in Massachusetts, opting for the mid-19th-century version of off-grid living.

Maybe you are tired of the commute, the cost of living, and the stress of city life. Perhaps Thoreau was tired of his era's version of the rat race, too. That's why he encouraged his reader to aim higher than the values of society, famously writing:

> I went to the woods because I wished to live deliberately, to front only the essential facts of life, and see if I could not learn what it had to teach, and not, when I came to die, discover that I had not lived. I did not wish to live what was not life [. . .] I wanted to live deep and suck out all the marrow of life, [. . .] and if it proved to be mean, why then to get the whole and genuine meanness of it, and publish its meanness to the world; or if it were sublime, to know it by experience, and be able to give a true account of it in my next excursion.

In this spirit, I feel privileged to have been able to share my "true account" of my own experience in the woods. Although my tips are purely practical; I'll leave the more spiritual and literary meditations to a master like Thoreau! I mention him now because I believe he started with the same dream in his heart which you feel stirring in yours right now. What will you do about it?

From the increasing popularity of off-grid living—and indeed from Thoreau's own brilliant words—it's clear people have sought after the benefits of off-grid living for hundreds of years. These benefits are peace, solitude, self-reliance, and simplicity. But do the benefits of living off-the-grid outweigh the hassles and the risks? I think so. Thoreau seemed to think so as well, writing in his conclusion:

> I learned this, at least, by my experiment; that if one advances confidently in the direction of his dreams, and endeavors to live the life which he has imagined, he will meet with a success unexpected in common hours.

Will it be worth it for you? There's only one way to find out, and that's to get started. I began this book by noting that going off-the-grid can mean different things to different people. To you, dear reader, I hope the lessons I've learned and shared might help you get closer to "success unexpected", whatever you may define it to be.

Did You Enjoy This Book?

You Can Make a Big Difference and Spread the Word!

Reviews are the most powerful tool I have to bring attention to "The Simple Life". I'm an independently published author. Yes, I do a lot of this work myself. This helps me make sure the information I provide is straight from the heart and from my experiences, without some publishing company dictating what sells. You, the readers, are my muscle and marketing machine.

You're a committed group and a loyal bunch of fans!

I truly love my fans and the passion they have for my writing and products. Simply put, your reviews help bring more fans to my books and attention to what I'm trying to teach.

If you liked this book, or any of my others for that matter, I would be very grateful if you would spend a couple of minutes and leave a review. It doesn't have to be long, just something conveying your thoughts. If you would go to the website where you purchased this book from and leave a review, it would be greatly appreciated.

If you hated this book, and think I suck, I would appreciate an email conveying your thoughts instead of writing a scathing review . . . that doesn't do either one of us any good.

References

For a list of the sources used in this book go to:

https://www.thesimplelifenow.com/offgridreferences

ABOUT THE AUTHOR

GARY COLLINS has a compelling background that includes military intelligence, Special Agent for the U.S. State Department Diplomatic Security Service, U.S. Department of Health and Human Services, and U.S. Food and Drug Administration. Gary's expert knowledge brings a much-needed perspective to today's areas of simple living, health, nutrition, entrepreneurship, self-help, and  being more self-reliant. He holds an AS degree in Exercise Science, BS in Criminal Justice, and MS in Forensic Science.

Gary was raised in the High Desert at the basin of the Sierra Nevada mountain range in a rural part of California. He now lives off-the-grid part of the year in a remote area of NE Washington State and spends the rest of the year exploring in his travel trailer with his trusty black lab Barney.

Gary considers himself lucky to have grown up in a small town where he enjoyed fishing, hunting, and anything outdoors from a very young age. He has been involved in organized sports, nutrition, and fitness for almost four decades. He is an active follower and teacher of what he calls "life simplification". Gary often says:

"Today, we're bombarded by too much stress, not enough time for personal fulfillment, and failing to take care of our health . . . there has to be a better way!"

In addition to being a best-selling author, Gary is a highly sought after speaker in numerous areas, as they relate to self-improvement and life simplification. He has taught at the University level, consulted and trained collegiate athletes, and been interviewed for his expertise on various subjects by CBS Sports, Coast to Coast AM, The RT Network, and FOX News, to name a few.

His website **www.thesimplelifenow.com**, podcast *Your Better Life,* and *The Simple Life* book series (his total lifestyle reboot), blows the lid off of conventional life and wellness expectations and is considered essential for every person seeking a simpler, and happier life.